Startup Power

An Entrepreneurial Guide to Starting Your Own Business

Jimmy Bayes, Ph.D.

Startup Power: An Entrepreneurial Guide to Starting Your Own Business

ISBN: 0-9965824-3-6
ISBN-13:   978-0-9965824-3-8

Printed in the United States

All communication or requests to the author should be sent by mail to Dr. J. D. Bayes, c/o Dunamis Empowerment Foundation at 1716 Briarcrest Drive Floor 3, Bryan, TX 77802 or electronically to director@dunamisempower.org.

This publication is designed to provide accurate and authoritative information regarding the subject matter covered. It is provided with the understanding that the author is not responsible for the results that may occur in applying the following information.

Dunamis Publications
Copyright © 2016
All Rights Reserved

DEDICATION

This book was written for and is dedicated to emerging entrepreneurs everywhere. My firm belief is that the entrepreneurial spirit lies within each of us. Some people are in touch with that spirit very early in life, change the world, and make millions of dollars. For others, such as myself, the inner entrepreneur takes a while to emerge. The good news for everyone is that entrepreneurship is an activity and a behavior, and as such, it can be learned and developed. This book was born from my passion to empower others so that they can claim more control of their lives.

CONTENTS

ACKNOWLEDGMENTS

I would like to acknowledge several people whom I owe many thanks. I would like to thank Dr. Winston and my professors at the School of Global Leadership and Entrepreneurship at Regent University for teaching me leadership and organizational development. I want to thank my coach, Iris Hainstock, for coaching me through the start of the workshops for emerging entrepreneurs. I would like to thank Erik Dombach and Jim Pillans for their insights into entrepreneurship and this book. I owe a debt of gratitude to Starla Akers for editing this work, Sierra Bayes for the cover design, and my wife, Michelle, for supporting me during this process. Finally, I would like to thank T. Getterman, Jacob Davis and Bart Monroe for their encouragement and help in my own entrepreneurial journey.

Introduction to startup power

The first iteration of this book was in the form of a manual for entrepreneurial workshops for emerging entrepreneurs. The purpose of the workshops is to inspire and teach basic entrepreneurial principles, to form a community of established and emerging entrepreneurs, and to start and grow businesses. It is important for an emerging entrepreneur to be a part of a network of entrepreneurs so that they can learn from each other. This book is also an extension of www.startuppower.co, a resource for entrepreneurs.

Many entrepreneurs make starting successful businesses look easy. These businessmen and women seem to be born entrepreneurs. However, entrepreneurs tell stories of the difficult times they experienced before achieving success. When we eat at their restaurants or go into their businesses, it is difficult to tell if they are struggling to stay open or if they are experiencing incredible growth. Even the so-called born entrepreneurs cannot escape the required hard work, the constant risk of failure, and the ever-changing market.

There have been enough entrepreneurial successes and failures to give a large amount of data to show good entrepreneurial practices and understand the pitfalls to avoid. Entrepreneurship is a behavior and a set of practices that can be learned and applied in any context. Even if you have never started a business, or thought about starting a business, the good news is that there is a process that can be learned.

The goal of this book is to communicate the basic principles required for any person to start their business venture, but beyond basic instruction, we hope to network with other entrepreneurs through social media and our website. One person alone cannot build a successful business. A successful startup requires a group of people or a team.

Many entrepreneurs refer to **entrepreneurial ecosystems**. An entrepreneurial ecosystem refers to the elements (people and organizations) outside the individual entrepreneur that are conducive to the choice of a person to become an entrepreneur, and the probabilities of their success. Many mid to large cities have entrepreneurial ecosystems made up of successful entrepreneurs who mentor emerging entrepreneurs. Many organizations are being established that serve as hubs or meeting places for the entrepreneurial person.

"**Tribe**" is also another term that has become popular in certain startup and success networks. A tribe is a group of people connected to one another, connected to a leader, and connected to an idea. A group needs only two things to be a tribe: a shared interest and a way to communicate. Startup Power is building an **entrepreneurial tribe**. This tribe is a network of entrepreneurial mentors and emerging entrepreneurs dedicated to helping one another bring their ideas to life and achieve success. Find more about entrepreneurial tribes at www.startuppower.co. You can also subscribe to Startup Power News and Updates.

1

Foundations of Entrepreneurship

The Importance of Entrepreneurship

Entrepreneurship is vital for stimulating economic growth and employment opportunities in every society.

According to the U.S. Small Business Administration, since the mid-1900's, small businesses have been credited with having 60 to 80% of the net new employment in the United States. In small economies, small businesses are the primary engine of job creation and poverty reduction.

The best way to boost economic recovery is to encourage higher levels of business creation. Job creation following nation-wide recessions stems from employment generated by small firms with fewer than 500 employees.

Entrepreneurship is the hope for America's youth and the best opportunity to bring people out of poverty.

What is Entrepreneurship?

Some have said that "entrepreneur" comes from the old French *entreprendre,* meaning to undertake. An entrepreneur is then, one who undertakes or manages. The early definitions of entrepreneurship describe the process of bearing the risk of buying at certain prices and selling at uncertain prices. This definition was subsequently broadened to mean the bringing together of factors necessary for production. From then until now, entrepreneurship has come to include risk taking, innovation, and starting companies.

There are many definitions of entrepreneur or entrepreneurship, but not one is universally accepted. There are many ideas of what entrepreneurship includes. Below are some randomly selected statements regarding entrepreneurship and entrepreneurs:

- Entrepreneurship is marketing a new or unique product or service.

- Entrepreneurship is a successful act of organizational founding.

- An entrepreneur is a person who organizes, operates, and assumes the risk for a business venture.

- An entrepreneur is a person who starts a new business or organization, taking some personal financial risk to do so.

- Entrepreneurship is the pursuit of opportunity without regard to the resources currently controlled.

- Entrepreneurship creates change and changes produce more opportunity for entrepreneurship.

- Entrepreneurship is the mind-set and the process to create and develop economic activity by blending risk-taking and creativity (and/or innovation) with sound management with a new or existing company.

- Entrepreneurs have a desire to found a private kingdom, drive to overcome obstacles, joy in creating, and satisfaction in exercising one's ingenuity.

- Entrepreneurs are individuals who are ingenious and creative in finding means that add to their wealth, power, and prestige.

- Entrepreneurship is the creation of new enterprise.

- Entrepreneurship involves all the functions, activities,

and actions associated with the perceiving of opportunities and the creation of organizations to pursue them.

- The entrepreneurial challenge is recognizing or generating ideas that have the potential to be developed into appealing goods or services.

- Entrepreneurs are decision-makers who improvise solutions to problems which cannot be solved by routine alone.

- An entrepreneur is anyone creating or running a startup (less than three months old) or a baby business (4 to 12 months old).

Who is an Entrepreneur?

There is not a profile for a successful entrepreneur, but many have identified characteristics common to most successful entrepreneurs. Although entrepreneurs do not have every one of these characteristics, they will exhibit many of them. An entrepreneur is...

- A person with a passion for starting their own business venture.

- A person with self-confidence (self-efficacy).

- A person with high self-esteem.

- A person capable of accomplishing things through sheer will.

- A person that is self-reliant.

- A person that is forward thinking (as opposed to those stuck in the past).

- A person willing to act upon a business idea.

- A person with vision and goals.

- A person with internal drive and motivation.
- A person willing to work hard.
- A person willing to take calculated risks.
- A person that is competitive.
- A person that is creative.
- A person that is willing to learn.

Additionally, many **entrepreneurial skills** have been identified:

- Ability to plan
- Good communication skills (writing and speaking)
- Marketing skills
- Interpersonal skills
- Basic Management skills
- Team building
- Leadership
- Wisdom (the ability to size things up)

The Four Main Characteristics of an Entrepreneur

While there are many opinions about the traits that successful entrepreneurs possess, there are some traits that are necessary. The following four characteristics are necessary for an individual to start and manage a successful business. These traits tend to be inherently possessed, but with help, they can be developed. Lacking these will hinder the entrepreneur's efforts.

Confidence

Confidence is the feeling or belief that you can do something well, or succeed at something. People have various levels of confidence, but it can be developed or strengthened. The best way for an emerging entrepreneur to develop confidence is to educate themselves in the entrepreneurial process, marketing and managing, and leadership. Learning is an important aspect of emerging entrepreneurs, the more the entrepreneur learns, the more confident they will become.

Emerging entrepreneurs need to surround themselves with other established and emerging entrepreneurs. Many communities are developing entrepreneurial ecosystems or tribes. Association with one of these entrepreneurship networks fosters confidence.

Emerging entrepreneurs should seek out mentors and hire a coach. Most entrepreneurs love to give back to emerging entrepreneurs. Even the most confident of new entrepreneurs need mentors and coaches.

Competence

Competence is having the required skill, knowledge, and the capacity to do things successfully. Starting a new business is not easy (or everyone would be doing it). However, there are known processes and knowledge that is needed to start organizations, and they can be learned.

An experienced entrepreneur once said, "Education is important for entrepreneurs, but school is not." Entrepreneurs must continually learn, even if they hold MBA or doctorate degrees from the most reputable schools. A level of competence and knowledge is needed for success, but it varies by industry, market, and product.

Courage

Courage is acting in the presence of fear and dread. Risk taking is an aspect of entrepreneurship present in most definitions of entrepreneurship. Entrepreneurs have the ability to summons the courage to take the necessary risk to start a business when success is not guaranteed.

The risks taken by entrepreneurs vary between each entrepreneur and each startup venture. The level of risk can be marked on a continuum somewhere between 1% risk and 99% risk. The higher the risk, the higher the amount of courage needed. The entrepreneur's task is to minimize the risk, especially if he or she intends to approach investors for startup capital.

Self-discipline

Business owners often insist that they are never off work. Even when they are home or on vacation, the burden of the company payroll, employees, sales, competition, etc. are on the owner's mind. Establishing a business and seeing it become a money-making venture, requires hard work and dedication. It cannot be stressed enough how hard it is to build a successful organization. It requires massive amounts of self-discipline. Self-discipline is the ability to control one's feelings and overcome one's weaknesses. Self-discipline is the ability to do what is necessary, regardless of how you feel.

Having a great amount of passion for the product, the process, or the mission dramatically increases the level of self-discipline. Olympic athletes exhibit incredible self-discipline to train for the chance at winning the gold medal. They have herculean levels of self-discipline because of the passion they have for their chosen sport and the possibility to compete and possibly achieve the highest reward for their efforts. Entrepreneurs should have a passion for their product/service, their business, or their mission.

Five Entrepreneur Roles

The job of an entrepreneur is not easy. Entrepreneurs undertake the task for many reasons, but mainly they start businesses for the challenge of success and success pays good dividends. However, entrepreneurs' must have knowledge in many areas of business and fulfill many roles.

Entrepreneurs' understand their strengths and weaknesses. They work in their strengths, continually develop their weaknesses, and build a team with people whose strengths compliment their weaknesses. An entrepreneur must wear at least five hats:

1. Visionary Leader

An entrepreneur starts a company because they have been inspired—for whatever reason—to start a business. The first job of the founder of the company is to develop and communicate their vision to their stakeholders, employees, and customers. Immediately, we think of entrepreneurs such as Bill Gates, Steve Jobs, and Warren Buffett who started from humble beginnings to inspire millions and effect the world. Small business owners may not have the influence of these billionaires, but they can have the same effect upon their sphere of influence.

2. General Manager

A general manager serves as the top executive for the startup and is responsible for strategy, structure, budgets, people and financial outcomes. In other words, in a startup, the entrepreneur's role as the general manager is in charge of everything. One of the founder's primary responsibilities is to fill necessary roles with competent people that share the founder's vision for the company.

3. HR Director

People are the most important resource for companies and the Human Resources department is an important division of every company. HR directors are responsible for the smooth and profitable operation of a company's human resources department. Typically, they provide consultation to management for employee hiring plans, compensation, benefits, training and development, budget, and labor relations.

4. Marketing Director

Marketing is the promotion, sales, and distribution of a product or service. Marketing covers a broad range of practices, including advertising, publicity, promotion, pricing, and packaging. The founder is the first person to market the product or service when he first pitches his idea to investors. After the startup launches into business, they begin pitching the service or products to customers.

5. Accountant

I have spoken to many startup owners that have said that financial mistakes are what caused their companies to fail. If the entrepreneur is not a professional bookkeeper or accountant, they need to hire a professional financial person before the startup launches into business.

Given the fact that the entrepreneur needs to have experience and expertise in communicating a vision, process and people management, marketing, and accounting they need to develop a startup team early in the process. I have known business owners that are good in two or even three of the areas, but I have not met an entrepreneur that is outstanding in all five areas necessary for starting a business. Work in your strength, develop your weakness, and surround yourself with others that compliment your strengths.

Why Become an Entrepreneur?

- Entrepreneurs give value to society by meeting needs and creating jobs.

- Entrepreneurs are their own bosses and gives the person unprecedented freedom.

- Being an entrepreneur and starting a business gives more control of your life.

- The rewards for starting your own business usually

outweigh the risks (with hard work and persistence).

- Entrepreneurs change the world.
- Nothing will develop you more than starting your own business.
- Starting your own business is fun and challenging.
- Why not start your own business?

Dealing with Failure

It is sad, but two out of every three businesses fail, some say nine out of ten fails. Other sources say that about 75% of new startup businesses do not make it past two years. Regardless of the numbers, starting a new business is difficult and not guaranteed.

Failure is nothing to be proud about, but it should not be the cause of a person's feelings of shame, especially because entrepreneurs say they learn more from their failures than they do their successes. In a recent podcast, a serial entrepreneur said that he has never experienced failure, but many of his businesses did not succeed. His point of view is that there is no failure in closing a business that is not taking off and starting another venture. Lost in the area of entrepreneurship is the fact that organizations have a life cycle. Although there are companies that have remained in business for decades, we must ask if organizations were meant to last forever especially in light to today's global competition, acquisitions, and mergers.

There are many reasons that startups fail. Reasons for their failure also reveal pitfalls to avoid. Below are 20 of the leading reasons for startup failure.

- Unclear need for product or service
- Ran out of cash
- Failure to assemble an effective team
- Cannot overcome competition

- Pricing and/or cost issues
- Poor product or service
- Inadequate business model
- Inadequate marketing
- Not listening to customers
- Poor market timing
- Loss of focus
- Internal conflict with team or external conflict with vendors or customers
- Incorrect adjustments (pivots)
- Lack of passion
- Lack of investment capital or investor interest
- Legal challenges
- Failure to network (do not use advisors, mentors and coaches)
- Burn out
- Failure to adjust (pivot)

2

Four Stages of Entrepreneurship

It has been said that entrepreneurship can be learned. While every entrepreneur, startup, and context will be very different, there are logical steps that entrepreneurs take in starting their businesses. There are at least four distinct phases of entrepreneurship. They are often cyclical and they develop and evolve over time. Also, one phase does not need to be completed before the next phase begins. In fact, it could be argued that the phases never come to an end during the life of the business.

Phase 1 – Idea Phase

Every startup business begins with an idea. Countless ideas for startup businesses have begun over coffee as entrepreneurs develop their new technology or service idea. Many ideas come out of an intense personal interest or talent. Some ideas begin by addressing a need. Some ideas are born in those unexplainable "ah-hah" moments, or when an entrepreneur spots an opportunity to exploit, while other ideas are deliberate attempts to innovate and impact the world. The characteristic that all good ideas share is creativity.

A good idea is a marketable idea. A marketable idea solves an existing problem or need, improves upon a current solution, or (in the case of Apple's iPod) creates an innovative solution before there is a problem. Addressing a few question will help identify a good idea.

What is the problem or need?

Society is wrought with problems waiting for solutions. Entrepreneurs that can address these problems become successful. Understanding society's physical, economic, social, and technological environments will help to reveal many problems.

After identifying a need, ask why the need exists. This void may be an opportunity that can be exploited.

What skill or talent do I have that can be used to address a problem?

Often entrepreneurs begin with a talent they have to address common needs. For example, women may choose to capitalize on their sewing or cooking skills to meet another's needs. Men may market their construction or mechanic skills to help others without such skills.

What is your proposition to address these problems and needs?

Regardless of whether you start by identifying a problem/need, or chose to begin with a skill or an ability, your proposition should address a problem or need that is identifiable.

Individuals often come up with good ideas that meet problems and needs, but more times than not, good ideas are formed by brainstorming with others. Even great innovative entrepreneurs like Steve Jobs need a group of people to help bring ideas to market.

Your solution to the identified problem and/or need will be either a product or service (P/S). A product is a producible item that can be manufactured or developed. Often these products are physical items that are produced for sale, but they can also be methodologies or programs.

What is unique about your propositions?

If answers to problems were simple or obvious, someone probably would have already addressed them. Your solution to the problem should be distinguishable from other available solutions (if any exist). If you want to capitalize on your cooking skills, you may want to open a restaurant. The need that is being addressed is simple—the need to eat. Whereas the competition in the restaurant business is large, the owner should distinguish their restaurant from existing restaurants.

Finally, articulate your "Big Idea"

State, in writing, your big idea. The statement should be a simple statement of what and why you propose what you are trying to do. The statement does not reveal your plan or strategy, this will be fully developed in your business and marketing plans.

Phase 2 – Data Phase

The "Big Idea" phase is the inspiration phase and the data gathering phase is the collecting knowledge phase. It is less creative and more time consuming. This phase helps to validate or invalidate your big idea. All of this data will be used when you begin to develop your business and marketing plans.

Data gathering is a big information dump. Begin by verifying the need or problem. Gather data that shows the extent and the depth of the problem. Gather data about existing solutions. Gather data about the targeted market. Examine the demographic data that applies to the industry. Read books and articles, listen to podcasts, talk to businessmen, view videos—learn all that you can.

Some startups require more data than others. Starting a factory for cookware will take more data than starting a lawn care business. Your goal in gathering data is clarity and understanding your market environment. You will need to be prepared for any question that will be asked by potential investors and employees.

Phase 3 – Strategy Phase

Once the need or problem has been identified, you have decided upon a product or service that addresses the problem, and you have collected as much data that pertains to your startup and its environment, it is time for the strategy phase.

The strategy phase answers the who, what, when, where, and how questions.

- Who will be involved in the startup? Having a team to help with the startup will give investors more confidence in the success of your business.
- What is the mission of the business? (What need does it meet?)
- What is the timeline for launching the startup? Develop a timeline with milestones.
- Where will the business be established?
- What are the business and marketing plans?

Phase 4 – Action Phase

This phase launches your business. You and your team have carried the idea of a business like an expecting mother carries a child, and now it is time to birth your business. If you have done your work carefully up to now, then you are ready to launch your business, and it begins the organizational cycle.

Understanding the Organizational Life Cycle

In his book, *"Predictable Success,"* Les McKeown identifies seven stages of organizational life. McKeown says that these stages are inevitable, and you cannot skip one to go to the other. However, he says that an organization can slide back and forth between stages.

Early Struggle – This is the preformation and birth of an organization that is marked by the struggle for cash flow and finding your niche in the market. The mortality rate in this stage is high and two-thirds of all startups do not survive this stage.

Fun – Your startup has broken through the early stages which is indicated by better cash flow and an established place in the market. Now you can breathe and have a little fun.

Whitewater – The seeds of success in the Fun Stage brings the seeds of Whitewater. The business is becoming more complex and the focus shifts from sales to profitability which requires processes, policies, and systems. The business is experiencing growing pains and a little identity crisis.

*Predictable Success – The team has navigated through the Whitewater stage and has reached the prime growth stage called Predictable Success. Goals are being set and reached with a predictable degree of success, and you know why the company has been successful. You use this information to sustain growth.

Treadmill – There is no reason that an organization must leave the stage of Predictable Success. However, too much reliance on the established policies and process causes the organization to become formulaic and arthritic. This stage can feel like being on a Treadmill requiring more and more effort with less and less progress.

The Big Rut – If the organization continues to the Treadmill Stage, it runs the risk of the dangerous Big Rut stage. If not checked in time, creativity, risk taking, and flexibility can be diminished or lost. At this stage, process and administration becomes more important than action and results and the organization loses its self-awareness and cannot see its own sickness. This stage can go for years in a steady decline.

Death Rattle – For all organizations, there is usually a final attempt to resuscitate the organization. Even with revival attempts, the organization will not survive in its present form (if it survives). Many organizations do not survive the death rattle.

The goal of an organization is to remain in the Predictable Success stage. There are five key characteristics of organizations that help them remain in the Predictable Success Stage:

Decision-making

Making good and timely decisions on the behalf of an organization is recognized as a defining characteristic of leadership. Jack Welch stated that his ability to make fast decisions without regrets is a defining quality of his leadership at General Electric.

Entrepreneurs' must make strategic decisions. However, not all leadership decisions are strategic. Some decisions are made conveniently because of familiarity. For example, an entrepreneur chooses to open a bank account because he is familiar with his personal bank's people and services—not because they give the best value for his company.

Some decisions are made by inference. An entrepreneur recognizes a similar situation and opts for the solution that worked in the similar situation. The decision may be good or bad, but it is not necessarily strategic. Strategic decisions anticipate future needs and select choices accordingly.

Some business guru's make a distinction between strategic decisions and tactical decisions. Strategic decisions are said to be long term, complex decisions made by senior management that will affect the entire direction of the firm. An example may be to become the market leader in their field. Tactical decisions are medium term, less complex decisions made by middle managers. Regardless of which adjective is used to describe the decision, they all must be foreword thinking and align with the overall vision, mission, and values of the company.

Decision-making tools are available like decision matrices and decision trees. A decision matrix considers choices plotted on two axis. The first measures the cost of the choices on a scale from \$0.00 to the highest estimated price. The second axis measures the benefit of the choice as high benefit or low benefit as determine by the decision team. Plotting each choice on a matrix will reveal the choice(s) that give the highest benefit at the lowest cost. The key is to weigh the cost against the benefit and compare choices. Regardless of the final choice, it is an informed decision and the entrepreneur or the entrepreneur's team will know the risk of each decision.

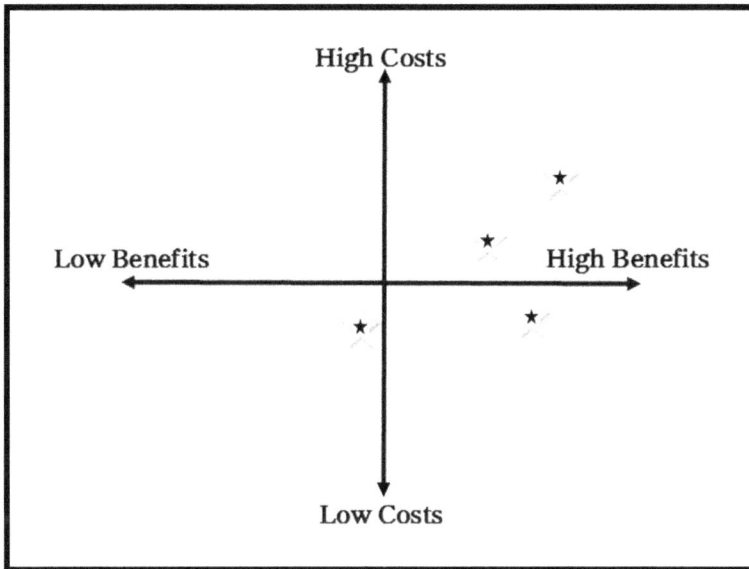

Decision trees are used when previous decisions are institutionalized. Decision trees do not work when facing a challenge not previously faced or when the organization is facing systemic change. All organizations use predetermined choices for many decisions and decision trees are good tools for determining these choices. Decision trees diagrams the possible choices and results so that the best decision can be made. Decision trees consist of previously determined questions or situations that are usually answered with a yes or no or they have a set of choices from which to select. Each answer leads to another choice until only one result is left. The final outcome depends upon the responses to each choice.

Goal Setting

The ability to readily set and consistently achieve goals is a mark of a successful entrepreneur. Goals give a company direction and motivation. The leadership team should set long-term and short-term goals. Goals, especially long-term goals, should be broken down into milestones. Milestones are important steps that are necessary for accomplishing goals. For example, building a new warehouse can be broken down into milestones of securing building funds, hiring an architect, selecting a plan, selecting a building contractor, and getting building permits. Each milestone should have a "complete by" date so that the project can stay on time.

Alignment

In his classic book, "The Fifth Discipline," Peter Senge wrote about systems thinking. System thinking sees the organization as a whole, not just individual parts. It is seeing interrelationships rather than things and seeing patterns of change instead of isolated events. Often the research and development department of companies do not communicate well with the marketing department. The result is the development of products the customer does not want or ignoring features that the customer desires. Systems thinking helps align the company where the organizational structure, process, and people are in harmony.

Accountability

Setting goals and identifying milestones are of little use if each employee and management team is not held accountable. Accountability is about having clear goals and roles. It is not about punishment, but about improvement. It is about evaluating expectations. First, each employee needs to be accountable to themselves and their personal role-specific goals, but there should be accountability among team members for job and organizational goals. Building a culture of accountability has each employee asking, "How can I become better?"

Ownership

Organizational experts often speak of employee engagement. Employee engagement is the extent to which employees feel passionate about their jobs, are committed to the organization, and put discretionary effort into their work. Employees engage the company not when they are told what to do and do it, but when they make company goals their own and personally strive to achieve them. When company goals become personal goals, they start to have ownership. Ownership doesn't mean you have an obligation to own the project. It doesn't mean you shouldn't involve others and go it alone. It means you feel an obligation to the results of the goals set by the organization and that you feel obligated to act on items that impact those goals.

3

Identifying the Market & Customers

There are two classifications of startup enterprises. The first, is the **Innovation Driven Enterprises**. The goal of many entrepreneurs is to change the world, or at least how people function in the world. These entrepreneurs are usually software developers or engineers. They desire to innovate and create by inventing or developing a new computer program, a new or more efficient product, or a superior service and have a global target. These startups require substantially more capital from investors. It is common for these companies to lose money the first few years, but make much more money in the long run through exponential growth.

The second type of startup is the **Small to Medium Enterprise**. The vast majority of startup businesses are small to medium companies. They most often serve a local economy (however, this has been changed by the internet). Sometimes referred to as a "mom and pop" business, they are also known as a "cottage industry." These businesses are often started out of a person's kitchen or garage. Small businesses have been credited with 60 to 80% of the net new employment in the United States. If you desire to start a large tech company to change the world or just a small local business to get more income, your company will need customers.

Customers are the most important aspect of entrepreneurship, but an often overlooked aspect. You don't have a business until you have paying customers. There have been countless stories of products being developed only to find out that prospective customers were not interested. Even the best and most innovative ideas are not good unless customers want to buy their products and services. Customer development should begin very early in the startup process; you do not want to waste valuable time and money on ideas that few people want. Whether starting a global innovation-driven business, or a local family run company, finding customers is the key to success.

Innovation driven startups need to target customer needs or their innovations will not be successful. *Innovation* is developing a new idea, method, or product to address existing problems. *Invention* is the creation of a new process or device. The difference between innovation and invention is customers. There is a formula for innovation: **I = I + C** (Innovation = Invention + Commercialization). Nikola Tesla invented the alternating current, the radio, the electric motor, and the laser among other inventions. However, he did not commercialize his inventions and died penniless. On the other hand, Thomas Alva Edison invented the incandescent light bulb, nickel-iron batteries, the phonograph, motion pictures, the electrographic vote recorder, and the magnetic Iron ore separator among others, but Edison was an innovator because he started a company and commercialized many of his inventions.

Product / Market Fit

Entrepreneurs should understand the markets in which they choose to operate. Igor Ansoff developed a strategic planning tool that offers a framework to help business men plan for future growth—the Ansoff Matrix. This matrix can be adapted to startup ventures. Every entrepreneur goes into business with a new or existing product/service (P/S) into a new or existing market. A different growth strategy should be used depending upon the combination.

When the entrepreneur is offering existing products or services in an existing market, they should use market penetration strategies such as competitive pricing, reliable P/S availability, and target non-users for example.

When the entrepreneur offers existing P/S in new markets, they should use market development strategies like market segmentation (marketing your P/S to a specific demographic within the larger market).

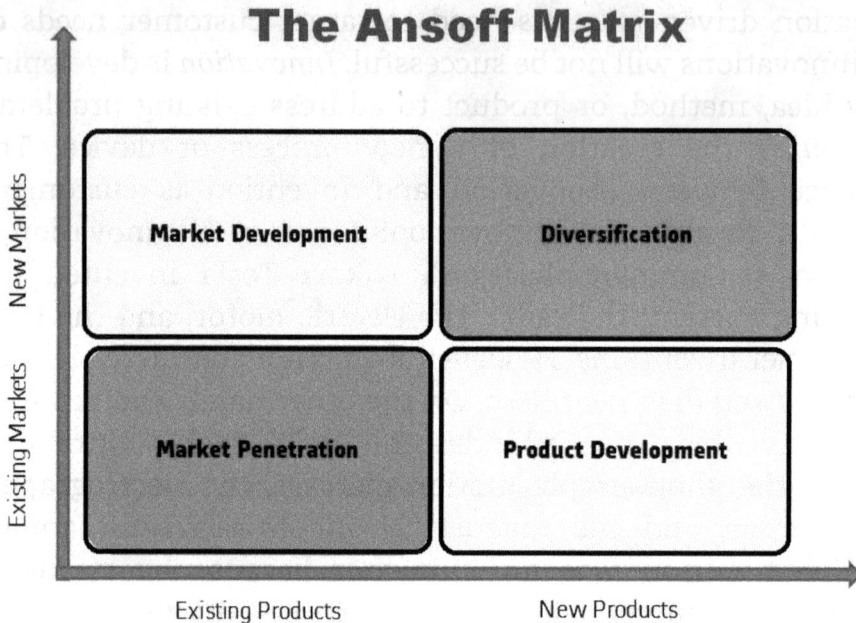

The Ansoff Matrix

	Existing Products	New Products
New Markets	Market Development	Diversification
Existing Markets	Market Penetration	Product Development

When the entrepreneur offers new P/S in existing markets, they should use product development strategies. Because the market already has the same or similar P/S, you must distinguish your P/S in some fashion like making a better P/S or customer service and excellence.

When the entrepreneur offers new P/S in new markets, they should use diversification strategies. This is the riskiest type of venture and takes much more advertising to penetrate a new market.

Understanding or choosing the right P/S—Market fit helps to develop hypotheses in the Customer Development phase.

Customer Development

Customer development is a vital component of every business and especially important to startups. A startup should have a defined product vision and then use a customer discovery process to find customers and define a market for that vision. There are four basic steps to customer development: customer discovery, customer validation, customer creation, and company building. This process is not just about getting customers, but it is about listening to customers and making changes in the product and/or delivery methods to serve customers better and to gain and retain customers. Customer development begins before the launch of the business, but must continue as the company matures.

Step 1: Customer Discovery

This step takes the entrepreneur's vision for the business and develops it into a set of hypotheses about each aspect of the product. These hypotheses are then tested by going directly to the customer and seeing if the hypotheses hold true. Having conversations with actual customers is critical. The entrepreneur must discover the needs of the customer and what features of the P/S they desire. Customer discovery is not about collecting a bunch of leads, but it is finding out what customers want directly from the customer.

A set of hypotheses that state the entrepreneur's vision for his P/S is developed. For example:

- I believe that {target market} will {do this action / use this product} for {this reason}.

- I believe that people in the downtown area will eat at our restaurant because of our location, menu, and prices.

Step 2: Customer Validation

Customer validation shows that the startup has been tested and is a repeatable, *scalable business model* that can deliver the volume of customers required to build a profitable business. If the hypotheses hold true at every point, the business can scale up. If the hypotheses are not true at any point, the entrepreneur must make a pivot. A pivot is a change. In our example, a pivot is a change in target customer, location, menu, or prices. Each pivot is tested in the same way.

During the customer validation stage, the business tests its ability to scale against a larger number of customers. After the customer validation phase, marketing and sales efforts should start in earnest.

Step 3: Customer Creation

Customer creation builds on the initial sales success of the company. Now the business accelerates its activities by spending money to drive customers into the sales channel or channels through marketing strategies.

Customer creation varies by each startup. Some startups capitalize on the already defined market by their competitors. Other startups will help to define their markets. Some startups segment the market and target a particular demographic. Each type of market demands different customer creation activates.

Step 4: Company Building

Reaching this step means that the startup has graduated into a full-fledged business. The business has made it through the early struggles, fun, and whitewater stages of development and hopefully enters into the predictable success stage. Now the organization needs to avoid the treadmill and ruts of dying businesses.

Customer Development Guidelines

1. Customer opinion comes from outside of the business, not from inside your business. You must talk directly

with your customer—don't guess about their opinion.

2. Customer Development is useless unless the business can adjust or pivot the product with speed and agility.

3. Failure is an expected aspect of customer development. If you are afraid to fail in a startup, you're destined to do so.

4. Be prepared to make continuous adjustments and pivots. They are essential to the customer development strategy.

5. No business plan survives the first contact with customers. Your business plan is dynamic and will change over time.

6. List your product and customer hypotheses and design experiments and tests to validate the hypotheses.

7. Agree on a P/S and market fit (see the Ansoff matrix page 24). This choice or understanding makes a difference in strategy.

8. The methods of measuring startups (metrics) differ from the methods of measuring existing companies. Startup metrics track the results of pass/fail tests of their hypotheses, and the forms of the business to which they lead. If a hypothesis fails, the entrepreneur makes a pivot to the business form. Each pivot resulting from hypothesis tests results in a different form or iteration of the business. Every business will go through several iterations before the company building stage.

    a. Have the customer problem and product features been validated?

    b. Do customers agree with the minimum features set by the startup?

    c. Who in fact is the customer?

    d. Have the initial customer related hypotheses (e.g. value of P/S to customer, sales channels, and target customer demographic) been validated through face-to-face customer validation?

    e.   Customer validation questions should include things like average order size and/or cost, product value to customer, average time from first contact to first order, and close rate. (Other metrics to measured are revenue per sale person, cash-burn rate, short-term hiring plans, and projected time till business reaches cash-flow break-even point.)

9.   Fast decision-making, cycle time (test/learn/pivot), speed and tempo are important for startups. Speed matters in startups where the bank account is declining each day. During the testing phase fast learning, building, stopping, or pivoting is crucial. Learning to make quick decisions is part of a successful startup.

10. Passion is paramount. A startup without driven, passionate people is dead the day it launches. Entrepreneurs are different types of people; they think differently. Each entrepreneur brings to the startup differing characteristics and traits, the one trait that they all must have is passion.

11. Job titles and functions are different from established companies because of their ad hoc nature.

12. Company leaders in startup business should be comfortable with uncertainty, chaos, and change.

13. Preserve all cash until needed—then spend strategically. The goal of customer development is not to avoid spending money, but preserving cash while searching for the repeatable and scalable business model. Once it is found, then spend freely. When money is tight, it is crucial to minimize wasteful spending.

14. Communicate and share the lessons. An important part of customer development is learning and discovery. The company should share everything that is learned outside the building with all the employees and stakeholders. These lessons should be kept as a narrative of the

business evolution available to those who have a vested interest in the business.

15. Customer development success begins with buy-in. For customer development to succeed, everyone on the team (founders, managers, engineers, marketers, salesmen, etc.) needs to understand and agree that the customer development process is vital to the success of the company. Everyone in the company needs to be on the same page so that any pivot will be understood and be successful. Customer development often changes every aspect of organizational function and metrics. Customer development reinvents the business model on the fly.

Final Words About Customers

I learned about the importance of customers working in grocery stores. One manager told me, in fact, that customers were king. Without customers, the grocery store is just a warehouse full of aging food items. The purpose of any business is to sell products or services to people willing to pay for them.

Businesses rely upon a satisfied customer base. A customer base is your repeat customers. A business grows by increasing its base. Customer development is about finding out what the customer wants so that they can increase first-time customers and retain them as repeat customers.

Marketing

Marketing is the process of researching, promoting, selling, and distributing a product or service. Marketing covers a broad range of practices, including advertising, publicity, promotion, pricing, and packaging. Startups are dead without a marketing strategy.

The business plan should include information obtained from a market analysis. A market analysis should include an overview of your industry, a look at your target market, an analysis of your competition, your own projections for your business, and any regulations you'll need to comply with. Much of the needed data is available on the internet at the U.S. Census Bureau, Business.gov, U.S. Small Business Administration, Bureau of Labor Statistics, Commerce.gov, and other sites.

A Marketing Plan is similar to the Business Plan and much of the marketing information is contained in the Business Plan. It is useful, however, to have a separate Marketing Plan. The following headings show the information included in a marketing plan. (See glossary for unknown terms page 86)

Marketing Plan
- Executive Summary
- Description of Company
- Company Mission and Goals
- Core Competencies
- Situational Analysis
- Market Competitors
- Targeted Market or Market Segment
- Marketing Mix
  - Product Strategy
  - Distribution Strategy
  - Promotional Strategy
  - Pricing Strategy
- Budgeting, Scheduling, & Monitoring of Advertisements

Advertising

Advertising is the act or practice of calling public attention to your business, product, service, or need, usually with paid announcements in newspapers and magazines, over radio or television, on billboards, etc.

An advertising campaign is developed by a business to encourage potential customers to purchase a good or service. An advertising strategy is usually tailored to a target audience within the community most likely to purchase the product. Advertising strategies include elements such as geographic location, demographics of the audience, price points, special offers, and what advertising media (such as billboards, websites, or television) will be used to present the product.

Return on Investment (ROI) is of prime importance in any advertising campaign. Advertising can become costly, especially for radio or television spots. Utilizing a decision matrix like the one on page 19 can help the entrepreneur or startup team decide upon the best forms of advertising.

4

Startup Methods

You feel that you have what it takes to start a successful business. You believe that you have an idea that is marketable, and you believe that you have identified a customer base, and now you have decided you want to start your business, but you are not sure of the process. This chapter gives the basic outline of two methods of starting a business. There are two kinds of entrepreneurship or startups. The entrepreneur should know what kind of startup they are building, before deciding upon which startup method to use.

Innovation Driven Enterprises are built upon an innovative technology or method intended on making a huge impact on society and have a global focus. Innovation driven startups are intended on being very large corporations, they require huge amounts of startup capital, and take a considerable time to launch and develop. The profit to loss ratio will be negative for a long time until they start earning a profit. Companies such as Google and Yahoo took years before they began to make money for their shareholders.

The second type of startup is the **Small to Medium Enterprise**. The vast majority of startup companies will remain small with a percentage of these becoming medium-sized. These enterprises are started by a single individual or a team of people. These startups are not usually intended to grow into large corporations (although some do), and their focus remains local. They hope to start making a profit from the time of launch.

Startup Methods

I am aware of one entrepreneur that just filed the necessary paperwork, opened a banking account, and started doing business. This entrepreneur's spouse had a large income and they did not need to worry about taking risks, raising capital, or developing a customer base; they just started a business. This is the exception to the rule. Most entrepreneurs need a plan to follow. Fortunately, startup methods have been established and validated. There are two general ways to start a business although there may be variations of them.

Investment Driven Startup

The typical startup method is aimed at raising startup capital and can be called Investment Driven Startup. Investment driven startups sell a vision or dream, and the purpose is to convince investors that they are the ones to realize the dream. There are five basic steps to the typical startup method.

Idea

Every startup begins with an idea for a marketable product or a service. See Idea Phase page 13 for more information.

Business Plan

The purpose of a business plan is to bring together the elements of your business in one document. Unless an entrepreneur is prepared to show potential investors a well-thought-out plan for making the business profitable, he won't have much chance convincing them to finance the venture. Even if the entrepreneur does not plan on presenting their startup idea to raise funds, the Business Plan document is still important to have. (See appendix B for a sample business plan.)

A Business Plan is important because

- It provides a blueprint for the entrepreneur and their team.
- It provides proof of the viability of your idea.
- It helps with goal-setting and long term planning.
- It helps explain the business to others.
- It helps explain and attract potential employees.

Each Business Plan varies according to the business and the investors sought. To develop your business plan more research should be done to determine the specifics needed to explain the startup plan fully. Each Business Plan is different, but a general Business Plan includes:

- Title Page
- Table of Contents
- Executive Summary
- Company Description
- Purpose of Company
- Description of Product or Service
- Analysis of Market
- Analysis of Competition
- Marketing & Selling Strategy
- Operating Plan
- Management Plan
- Financial Projections
- Supporting Documents

A Business Plan may also include:

- The need for capital
- Sources of Financing

- Description of Intellectual Property
- Strengths of a Small Business
- Business Accomplishments
- Break-even Analysis
- Profit/loss forecast
- Startup Cost Estimates
- Cash Flow Projections
- Exit Plan for Investors

Raising Capital

Once the Business Plan is complete, you are now ready to present your startup idea to investors.

- First, obtain leads and referrals of the type of investors you seek.

- Research your target investors. Learn as much as possible about how much they typically invest, to whom they typically give, what interests the investors have, and other requirements.

- Make your pitch. Send an introductory email or letter stating that you have a plan. A letter of introduction is your way of asking them if they would be interested in reading your business plan. Include in the introductory communication: your elevator speech, why they were selected, what kind of investment you are looking for, a referral list if any, the terms you are seeking, and if they are to be the sole investors or if there may be others. If you don't hear from them in a week send another, wait a week and send another. If three correspondeces do not result in a response, look elsewhere.

- Try to get person to person meetings. Not all investors are willing to hear a personal plea for funds. Because passion is an important part of the entrepreneur's presentation, a personal presentation is best.

- Defuse objections. Always be prepared and do your homework before presenting your plan to investors. Brainstorm with your startup team or advisors to anticipate every question that the investors may ask and rehearse them before the presentation is given.

- Get a commitment. You will not get an investment unless you ask for it. When all of the objections and questions have been addressed, offer one last concession for example, "If I give your representative a board seat (or advisory position), can we do this today?" Then go for the close.

Forbes.com gives eight mistakes that entrepreneurs make when pitching to investors:

1. The elevator speech is longer than one minute. There is nothing more powerful than to succinctly communicate your business plan, strategy, and goals in 60 seconds with passion.

2. The PowerPoint presentation is too long. Remember that potential investors likely listen to presentations daily. The presentations that are short, to the point, and communicate the most important facts will keep their attention. The PowerPoint should be no longer than 12 to 15 slides.

3. Not having a factually well-written business plan and/or executive summary. It is imperative that the presentation is free of error. If the business plan has mistakes, incorrect or inadequate information, they will not trust you with their investment money.

4. Not including a realistic exit strategy for investors. An investor is thinking about how they can make the greatest amount of money in the shortest amount of time. The exit strategy for the investor is getting their investment back with interest. Avoiding this reality is to ignore the investor's primary interest.

5. Asking for a non-disclosure agreement. Because investors listen to proposals so often, they probably have heard or will hear similar propositions. They see little need for signing these agreements. Also, signing them just opens them up to potential law suits. Most investors are professional and non-disclosure agreements are unnecessary.

6. Submitting investment proposals in mass. Investors should be given the respect to have individual proposals.

7. Discussing the return on their investment too early in the negotiations. Wait for the investor to begin the discussion of valuation and pricing.

8. Failure to listen to investors. Always be open to investors suggestions, lack of humility will not endear you to investors.

Launching the Business

Once you have successfully raised the money required for your startup as outlined in your Business Plan, you are ready for launch. The Business Plan gives you an outline for launching the business including the location, marketing, sales channels, etc. Much of the preliminary work has already been done, but now is the time to present your product to your customers.

Manage and Grow the Business

Once the company starts, the entrepreneur is now primarily a manager. It is up to them to gather loyal and talented people to help them grow the company. See the "Action Phase" and "Understanding the Organizational Life-cycle," page 16.

Hypotheses Driven Method (The Lean Startup)

I refer to the second method of startup as the Hypothesis Driven Method (HDM), but it is more commonly referred as the Lean

Startup. In the HDM, entrepreneurs translate their vision into verifiable business model hypotheses, and then test the hypotheses using a series of minimum viable products (MVP). A MVP is the smallest thing you can build to deliver the value of your solution to your customers.

Each of the MVPs represents the smallest set of features or activities needed to rigorously validate a concept. Based on feedback from the tests, entrepreneurs must then decide whether to persevere with their business model, to pivot by changing some model elements, or to abandon the startup. Although not necessary, I suggest that entrepreneurs using the HDM method develop a Business Plan for use as a dynamic internal roadmap..

The concept behind HDM is to apply the scientific method to a set of hypotheses made regarding each MVP in a representative batch of the business model. A MVP is the product which has just enough features to gather validated learning about the product and its development.

MVPs don't need to be actual products. A MVP is simply the quickest thing you can make to learn about your next most pressing hypothesis. Here are some examples of MVPs for an online business.

- A landing page explaining the product with a "Buy" button, and an Adwords campaign.
- A survey to identify how many people would pay for my app.
- A demo video highlighting the differences between existing products and your product.

Once the MVP(s) are identified, hypotheses are made regarding each MVP, tested, proven right or wrong, pivots made or persevere with the current model. A validation model of **build→measure→learn** is applied to each hypothesis.

Testing of each MVP reveals information about them, but you must know what kind of information you are wanting. Before testing each MVP, three questions should be asked.

1. What are you wanting to learn with this MVP?
2. What data is being collecting about your experiment?
3. What determines the success or the failure of your experiment?

The point of this exercise is to determine if your representative product is valuable to the customer and a viable commodity that can be expanded or built upon to form a successful business.

The HDM process

1. Start with an idea for a marketable product or service that is packaged into a testable scenario.

2. List what must be true for your idea to be successful.

   • Example: "A problem […] exists and the current solution is […], but I have a unique solution […] that is better than the alternative that is currently being bought because […].

3. Figure out how you will prove or disprove these hypotheses using small batches in a minimum amount of time.

4. Did you prove or disprove the hypotheses? Is it time apply more resources? Do you need to reformulate and retest?

5. →Pivot Loop – Depending upon the lessons learned from the tests, you have two options: (a) pivot or (b) continue with plan. A pivot corrects the original hypothesis and starts the process over, adjusting the original idea (#1),

then establish new hypothesis (#2), and then testing the new hypotheses (#3 & #4). This process continues until all hypotheses are proven, and then go to the next step (#6).

6. Persevere or continue with the business plan.

There are many examples of successful lean startup companies at *http://theleanstartup.com/casestudies*.

HDM verses the Investment Driven Startup Models

HDM startup is about experimentation and learning. It's about going slow before going fast. The Investment Driven Model is about selling the business ideas (in the form of a business plan) to raise startup funds then starting full bore.

5

Financing, Branding, & Registering Startups

Perhaps the most difficult aspect of starting a business is raising startup funds. The entrepreneur will want to determine if the business will generate the type of income needed or desired. A **pro-forma income statement** is often used to make this determination. (Pro-forma income statements are often generated on an Excel spreadsheet.) This statement is based on a set of assumptions and projections. A determination of estimated startup capital is needed regardless of what startup method is used. This estimation should include one-time costs, reoccurring costs, and the cost of all assets needed to launch the business.

Step 1 - Determine Startup Expenses

Think of startup expense as one-time expenses needed to start your business. Startup expenses are incurred prior to selling your product or service. They include any legal fees, branding fees (logo, web-design, etc.), insurance, licenses or permits, rent and security deposits, office supplies, training, software, consultant fees, legal and accountant fees, pre-opening marketing and advertising fees, and other miscellaneous fees. Note: after the business starts, expenses are accounted for in the profit-and-loss statement.

Step 2 - Determine Startup Asset Costs

Assets are tangible things like tables, chairs, land, and equipment. They are also things such as intellectual property. Assets are not deductible against income. However, assets whose value decline over time can be depreciated. After the business starts, list the assets on the balance sheet. Assets usually include cash in the bank, starting inventory, land and buildings, office furniture and equipment, signage, and leasehold improvements.

Step 3 – Estimate Reoccurring Expenses

One of the hardest estimates is the cash needed in the bank (cash reserve) to keep the business afloat during lean months. Most businesses experience a lean period after they open until they can to develop a reliable customer base. Recurring expense (usually monthly expenses) include rent, utilities, payroll, inventory, marketing, and other miscellaneous expenses.

Determining Startup Costs Worksheet

Startup Expenses

Legal/Accounting	$
Branding/Internet	$
Registrations (DBA, etc.)	$
Prelaunch Advertising/Marketing	$
Prelaunch Insurance	$
Deposits	$
Consulting Fees	$
URL/software	$
Misc. Startup Costs	$

Needed Assets

Cash	$
Inventory	$
Equipment	$
Land	$
Building	$
Office Equipment	$

Signage	$
Improvements	$
One Time Misc.	$

Recurring Expenses

Rent/Leases	$
Utilities	$
Phone/Internet	$
Advertising/Marketing	$
Salaries	$
Insurance	$
Operating Costs	$
Maintenance	$
Postage/Shipping	$
Office Costs Misc.	$
Taxes	$

Summary

The next step in starting a business, after you figure out how much it will cost, is to determine from where the money will come. It is also a good idea to develop a business plan. A good business plan can help you explain what you are trying to accomplish, how you are going to accomplish it, describe what or who will be involved in the enterprise, and your needs in moving the business forward. Business plans can take many forms, but they usually contain the same basic information. (See appendix B for a sample business plan.)

Startup Valuation

Sooner than later, the entrepreneur will be asked how much their startup is worth. The worth of a company is especially important to investors. It is a difficult task to value a company that has been in operation for years, and even more difficult to value a company that has not entered the market. There are several methods to value a company, but there is not an universally accepted method. Some of the methods are complicated and each of them are based on speculation.

One method is based on what it would cost business men to duplicate the business. The idea is that investors should not spend more than what the company would cost to duplicate. Another method of valuation is based on the value of a recently acquired business that is similar in a similar market. This is good information if the details of the sale of a similar business is available. A third valuation method is based on cash flow. However, this information is not available to startup businesses. In these cases, value lies in the future potential cash flow. Discounted cash flow analysis, then, represents an important valuation approach. *Discounted Cash Flow* is a valuation method that involves predicting how much cash flow the company will produce in the future, and then, using an expected rate of investment return, then calculating what that cash flow is worth. A higher discount rate is typically applied to startups, as there is a high risk that a company will inevitably fail to generate sustainable cash flows.

One valuation method often used by investors bases the value of a startup on the stages of development. The value of each stage is generally set by the investors. The typical stages of development look something like:

1. The owner has an exciting business idea or business plan.
2. The owner has a strong management team in place to execute the plan.
3. The owner has a final product or service or prototype.
4. The owner has strategic alliances or partners.

5. The owner has a customer base or signs of a customer base.

6. The owner has clear signs of revenue potential.

7. The owner has an obvious pathway to profitability.

The more positive the response to these statements increases the potential value of the company. Investors often look at other factors such as being in a hot industry, having experience in a similar business, having a proven product or service, and gaining traction in the startup process.

Determining Potential Income

The prime objective of every startup is to generate income. Potential investors will be interested in the income projections of your company. Often emerging entrepreneurs assume that their previous experience in a given area will be to get investors to write you a check. You may be an expert in your field, but investors want to know what your income potential will be. It is relatively easy to estimate the earning potential of your company. However, it should be noted that even the best projections are a guess at best. First, the entrepreneur should be able to answer some basic questions about their product or service.

1. What product or service will you provide?
2. How many different products or services will be offered?
3. How much will it cost to produce or develop the products/services?
4. What are your other expenses not related to producing the product or service (fixed and variable costs)?
5. What is the unit cost of your product or service?
6. How many units per month will your company sale?
7. What is the selling capacity per month?

It is difficult (if not impossible) to answer each of these

questions before entering the market, but your initial income projections depend on the answers. Some companies offer many products or services, and others only offer a few products or services. The more products or services a company have for sale, increases the income potential.

Having a realistic picture of the earnings, requires an understanding of accounting terms such as gross income, net income, variable costs, fixed costs, overhead, etc. Simplistically, gross income is all money made from sales of the company after the cost of selling the product is deducted. And net income is all the revenue made after the taxes and interest is subtracted. See the example below:

Total Income	20,000.00
Cost of Goods Sold	(10,000.00)
Gross Income	10,000.00
Gross Income	10,000.00
Operating Expenses	(5,000.00)
Earnings before Taxes/Interest	5,000.00
Earnings before Taxes/Interest	5,000.00
Taxes	(1,000.00)
Interest	(1,000.00)
Net Income	3,000.00

Where to Find Investors

When you have a firm business plan in place. It's a good time to start finding startup capital. To find investors, consider the following:

- Attend professional networking events.
- Reach out to other entrepreneurs.

- Consult a local company, organization or university for resources such as consulting and startup cash.

Research whether your city has an angel network or any angel investors. Angel investors are often people willing to invest in startups, but usually want more of a stake in the venture. Their help includes not only money but also advice and guidance as well. While angel investors may offer less cash than venture capitalists, the chances of attracting angel investors are more likely as you take the time needed to prove yourself and your idea.

As always, get it in writing. A promissory note states the terms, rights, and obligations of the loan. That includes the loan amount, interest rate, repayment terms and other needed provisions.

Family and Friends

Family and friends may provide you with smaller loans when you are finding startup capital. You can get money quicker and without as many contractual strings. There are still risks, however.

Even with family and friends, make sure you have a solid business plan in place. Do your homework, and make sure your business is at the business stage and not the idea stage. Make sure there's a benefit such as interest on the money they invest, and, regardless of whether they are family and friends, have all parties sign a promissory note.

Borrow Money

Entrepreneurs have to decide if they want to take on debt or use their own money. Most startups are funded with some form of debt. When borrowing, make sure to put all terms in writing. This goes for whatever the source. Read over the terms carefully to make sure you agree and seek legal advice if needed.

Community banks may be flexible to lend budding

entrepreneurs some startup cash. You can also borrow money by getting an asset-backed loan, such as a home equity line of credit, or apply for a Small Business Administration-backed loan.

Government Sources

When finding startup capital, use the SBA's Loans and Grants Search Tool to find a list of financing programs for which you may qualify. These include low-interest loans, venture capital, and scientific and economic development grants offered by federal, state and local governments. Government-backed grants are limited but may exist for very specific groups, organizations or activities, including businesses involved in scientific research.

Credit Cards

Credit cards are the most common way a business is financed. Going this route requires being comfortable with the interest payments and credit requirements.

Credit cards are a good resource because they are:

- Fast
- Able to be used as needed
- Able to be paid back when desired (to avoid unnecessary interest)

Credit cards typically have more expensive interest rates than you will find with other types of loans. If going this route, look for the best rates. Consider options including unsecured credit-line alternatives offered by Visa and American Express.

Angel Investors

An angel investor or angel (also known as a business angel, informal investor, angel funder, private investor, or seed investor) is an affluent individual who provides capital for a business start-up, usually in exchange for convertible debt or ownership equity. A small but increasing number of angel investors invest online through equity crowdfunding or organize themselves into angel groups or angel networks to share research and pool their investment capital, as well as to provide advice to their portfolio companies. Search the internet for sources.

Venture Capitalists

A venture capitalist is an investor who either provides capital to startup ventures or supports small companies that wish to expand but do not have access to equities markets. Search the internet for sources.

Crowd Funding

Crowdfunding or crowdsourcing is the practice of funding a project or venture by raising many small amounts of money from a large number of people, typically via the Internet. The concept behind crowd funding is to raise money from a large group of people instead of one or two major investors. There are several crowdfunding websites (https://www.gofundme.com and http://www.indiegogo.com).

Branding Your Business

Branding is creating a name, a logo, and message that identifies and differentiates your product or service from others. An effective brand strategy gives you a major edge in increasingly competitive markets. Branding goes beyond advertising gimmicks. A company brand can provide continuity and alignment within the company and communicate the purpose and essence of the company to the public.

Developing Your Company Brand

A company brand communicates your purpose and message to customers. A brand is developed by asking basic questions about the company.

- What is the purpose and mission of the company?

- What are the core values of the company?

- What message do you want to deliver to the customers?

- What qualities to you want customers to associate with your company?

- Write down the brand message that communicates this information.

Once this information is established in the entrepreneur's mind or with the startup team, the brand can be created. Branding goes beyond visually appealing graphics and clever advertising. Branding should think about the customer experience.

- Develop a brand name (if the company does not already have a name).

- Develop a unique brand logo.

- Develop a brand tagline or motto.

- Develop brand standards (design, color scheme, font, etc.) to insure visual continuity.

Communicate Your Brand

- Be conscious of the customer's experience.

- Be true to your brand.

- Be consistent in communicating the brand message.

- Be "brand conscious" within the company.

- Be visible. ("Visibility is credibility.")

- Have a market presence, but allow the customer to discover you.

A good brand:

- Promotes Company Recognition

- Sets Your Company Apart

- Reveals Your Company DNA

- Provides the Nucleus for Company Alignment

- Gives Your Company Meaning and Motivation

- Generates Referrals

- Communicates Customer Expectation

- Creates Clarity and Focus Within the Company

- Helps Connect to the Customer Emotionally

- Provides Company Value

Registering Your Business

Assumed Name Certificate

Some state and local governments require companies to register any alternate names under which they do business called a "Doing Business As" (DBA) filing. This action allows your company to operate legally under a trade name. This is sometimes referred to as an "assumed name."

Each state may vary in its business name requirements. In the state of Texas, proprietorships, general partnerships, and joint ventures are required to file an assumed name certificate with the county clerk in each county in which a business office is maintained or in each county in which the person conducts business. Some states do not require this and the entrepreneur should check their state requirements for starting a business.

Legal Structure

A major step in starting a business is to choose the best legal form for your new business venture. Often first-time entrepreneurs wonder what form of business structure they should have. A sole proprietorship seems convenient, but a corporation or LLC offers protection from personal liability. A rule-of-thumb is to focus energy and money on getting the business off the ground as a sole proprietorship or a partnership, you can always incorporate or form an LLC later. However, legal or professional counsel should be sought.

Sole Proprietorship

Most new businesses are sole proprietorships because: (a) it's normally the easiest and least costly way to organize, (b) it does not require formal legal papers, and (c) it does not require a separate tax return (a separate Schedule C is attached to your personal tax return—1040).

A sole proprietorship is simply a business owned by one person and that has not filed papers to be a corporation or an LLC. In the eyes of the government, a sole proprietorship is not legally separate from the person who owns it. This is a fundamental difference between a sole proprietorship and a corporation or LLC.

Under a sole proprietorship, the business is not transferable to others and is limited to the life of the proprietor. Also, there is no legal distinction between personal and business debts. The business itself is not taxed. The IRS calls this "pass-through" taxation, because business profits pass through the business to be taxed on the business owner's tax return.

It is important to understand that the business owner can be held personally liable for any business-related obligations. If the business doesn't pay a vendor, if it defaults on a debt, or loses a lawsuit, you can be forced to pay personally.

Partnership

The next step up the ladder is a partnership or general partnership. A partnership exists when two or more people join to operate a business. General partners are personally liable for all business debts, including court judgements. Each partner can be sued for the full amount of any business debt, though one partner can sue the other for their share of the debt. Any individual partner has "agency authority" and can bind the company to a contract or business deal.

Limited Liability Partnership

A Limited Liability Partnership is an alternative to a general partnership. An LLP is more appealing for many businesses because of the concern over unlimited liability for all partners in a general partnership. The limited liability partnership is similar to the general partnership, but each partners' unlimited liability may exclude obligations resulting from the professional mistakes made by the other partners. The partners are responsible for all claims and liabilities resulting from all other partnership activities.

A limited liability partnership requires at least one general partner and at least one limited partner. The general partner controls the company's day-to-day operations and is personally liable for the business. The limited partner has minimal control over business decisions or operations, and normally cannot bind the partnership to business debts. In return for giving up management power, a limited partner gets the benefit of protection from personal liability.

It is not legally necessary for a partnership to have a written partnership agreement in Texas (each state has different requirements). However, only with a clear written agreement will all partners be sure of the important details of their business arrangement. The partnership agreement can be structured so that your relationship can be however you want. It will establish the profits each partner will receive, the responsibilities of each partner, and what happens if any partner leaves.

Corporation

A corporation is the most complicated form and costly form of business structure. The corporation safeguards the business owner's personal assets. In forming a corporation, prospective shareholders exchange money, property, or both, for the corporation's capital stock. A corporation takes the same deductions as a sole proprietorship to figure its taxable income. A corporation can also take special deductions. A corporation conducts business, realizes net income or loss, pays taxes and distributes profits to shareholders.

The profit of a corporation is taxed to the corporation when earned, and then is taxed to the shareholders when distributed as dividends. This creates a double tax. The corporation does not get a tax deduction when it distributes dividends to shareholders. Shareholders cannot deduct any loss of the corporation.

To form a corporation, appoint the initial directors of your corporation. File formal paperwork, usually called "articles of incorporation," and pay a filing fee that ranges from $100 to $800, depending on the state where you incorporate. Create corporate "bylaws" which lay out the operating rules for your corporation.

From a taxation standpoint, there are two corporate forms:

C Corporations

A C-corporation, under the United States federal income tax law, refers to any corporation that is taxed separately from its owners. A C corporation is distinguished from an S corporation, which is not taxed separately.

- Its maximum tax rate is significantly lower than for individuals.

- The shareholders are not taxed personally for profits, nor do they benefit from any loss.
- The owners pay personal tax on any salaries and dividends. The bad news is that dividends are taxed twice—once to the corporation and again to the individual.

<u>S Corporations</u>

S corporations are corporations that elect to pass corporate income, losses, deductions, and credits through to their shareholders for federal tax purposes.

Shareholders of S corporations report the flow-through of income and losses on their personal tax returns and are assessed tax at their individual income tax rates. This allows S corporations to avoid double taxation on the corporate income. S corporations are responsible for tax on certain built-in gains and passive income at the entity level.

Limited Liability Company (LLC)

A limited liability company (LLC) is the United States-specific form of a private limited company. It is a business structure that combines the pass-through taxation of a partnership or sole proprietorship with the limited liability of a corporation.

Owners of an LLC are called members. Most states do not restrict ownership, and so members may include individuals, corporations, other LLCs and foreign entities. There is no maximum number of members. Most states also permit "single-member" LLCs, those having only one owner.

A few types of businesses generally cannot be LLCs, such as banks and insurance companies. Each state may use different regulations, and you should check with your state if you are interested in starting a Limited Liability Company.

Deciding On a Business Structure

There is not a way to figure out what type of legal structure is best for your business, nor is there a check list or a decision tree (although one could be made). However, there are several aspect to consider while determining the structure of a new startup company.

Size and Scope of the Company

If the entrepreneur hopes to create a company with a large vision and global reach, then he should incorporate the business. If the company remains small with a local focus, then a sole proprietorship or partnership will be adequate.

Number of Founders

If there are more than one founder, they have the choice of incorporating or forming a partnership.

Taxation

If the startup remains little more than an individual getting paid for a small service or product, it matters little if the IRS views their taxes as one entity. When an individual is taxed instead of the business, it is called "flow-through" taxation. A flow-through entity (FTE) is a legal entity where income "flows through" to investors or owners; that is, the income of the entity is treated as the income of the investors or owners. Sole Proprietorships, Partnerships, and S Corporations are flow-through entities.

Liability

The bad news about Sole Proprietorships and General Partnerships is that the owner(s) are liable for any law suit brought against the company. Owners are protected from legal actions in Limited Liability Companies, Limited Liability Partnerships, and Corporations.

LLC's provide more protection in terms of shielding personal assets from the operations and debts of the business. With an LLC there is a 100% separation between the two and personal assets are protected (unless an owner has committed fraud or committed other crimes via the LLC).

LLP's provide protection from the actions and debts of your fellow partners, with your personal assets not being protected from any actions or debts you may take on yourself. As such there is less protection of personal assets in an LLP.

One of the main advantages of incorporating is that the owners' personal assets are protected from the corporation's creditors. For instance, if a legal judgment is entered against the corporation stating that it owes a creditor $50,000, you cannot be forced to use personal assets, such as your house or land, to pay the debt. Because only corporate assets need be used to pay business debts, you stand to lose only the money that you've invested in the corporation.

Employee Identification Number (EIN)

An employer identification number (EIN) is a nine-digit number assigned by the IRS. It is used to identify the tax accounts of employers and certain others who have no employees. The IRS uses the number to identify taxpayers who are required to file various business tax returns. They are easily obtained online at *www.irs.gov.*

6

Launching Your Business

This chapter lists the basic steps of starting a business. As we have seen, and have been listed below, there are many steps, many options, and many details to starting a business. This book is a good place to start, but nothing can replace your personal research.

The success or failure of your business largely hangs on the decisions you make. Entrepreneurs' should have a have a decision-making process, especially if the decisions are a team effort. There are many **decision-making** models, but each one should include these step (see more about decision-making page 19).

1. Identify Decision Objective

2. Gather Information

3. Identify Options

4. Weigh the Evidence

5. Choose from the Options

6. Take Action

7. Evaluate the Results

Evaluation of each decision is important, but often neglected. A perfect decision is rare. Almost all decisions can be improved upon with small adjustments. When the decision does not work satisfactorily or not at all, the entrepreneur needs to make a business pivot. A pivots is a change in strategy, but implies keeping one foot firmly in place as you shift the other in a new direction.

Getting Started on Your Business

While there are certain steps that every startup business must do, there is not a specific order in which they must be completed. However, some steps must be completed before others can be done. For example, fund raising can be started before a business plan is developed and a building could be leased before your big idea is developed, but it is not advised. Some of the steps can be worked on simultaneously. Product development and company branding can be developed at the same time. This section lists the steps in the basic order that most startup companies follow.

You have raised enough capital to launch your business. You have the cash to launch your business fully or you are ready to test a set of hypothesis and build your customer base. Following are a set of items that are basic to most new businesses. Every state has different requirement for starting a business. However, most of them are the same or similar.

Note: The items below do not include some of the specifics already covered including product development, market analysis, and customer development. They will be covered in the Business Plan which will be a roadmap for your business.

A word of caution: Before launching your business, do your research to find out the specific legal requirements in your area.

The following steps are intended to give the entrepreneur a step-by-step guide to starting their business. Purchase a notebook and work through each of these steps. A checklist is also provided beginning on page 62.

Develop a Marketable Product or Service (P/S)
- Develop Your Big Idea
- Do a Feasibility Study & Business Plan
- Prepare to Pitch Idea to Stakeholders

Recruit People
- Build a Team
- Find Investors
- Identify a Customer Base

Brand Your Product or Service
- Articulate the Values of Your P/S
- State Why Your P/S is a Better Value Than Others
- Show the Competitive Advantage of Your P/S

Prepare Your Market
- Conduct a Market Analysis
- Begin Customer Validation / Development
- Identify Competing Providers of Similar P/S

Decide on a Business Model
- Choose Sales Channels
- Write Business Plan
- Develop Launch Blueprint with Dates and Milestones

Decide & Register a Legal Structure
- Decide Upon a Business Type
- Decide Upon a Business Name (DBA)
- Get Federal Employment Identification Number (EIN)

Execution
- Go to Market / Execute the Plan
- Marketing / Advertising

- Sales / Customer Service

Financial

- Leases / Contracts
- Insurance
- Bookkeeping / Accounting
- Financial Statements / Taxes

Legal Issues

- Zoning
- Permits
- Regulations
- Payroll
- Employer Responsibilities

Addendum: Startup Checklist

There are many steps to starting a business. Many of the main steps have been discussed, but there are many more that have not been addressed. We include here a checklist for starting a business. There are frequent changes in policy and legislation, so some of the steps may be different. Some of them may not apply depending upon the location and the industry that includes your startup. You are advised to seek professional guidance to verify that your business meets all the legal requirements before you start and operate your business.

- ☐ Choose a marketable product or service.

- ☐ Conduct in-depth research on the industry and the market.

- ☐ Write a business plan.

- ☐ Write a marketing plan.

- ☐ Register an Internet domain name even if you are not ready to use it.

- ☐ Select the office space (home or leased space).

- ☐ Check zoning laws and deed restrictions especially when operating a home-based business.

- ☐ Determine which legal form of business structure best meets your business needs.

- ☐ Register your Assumed Name Certificate or "Doing Business As" in the county where your business operates (if you are operating as a sole proprietorship).

- ☐ Verify your business name with the Secretary of State.

- ☐ File partnership, corporate, or LLC papers with the Secretary of State.

☐ If a corporation or LLC, obtain filing requirements for the state franchise tax (TX). Check your own state's laws.

☐ Apply for a Federal Employer Identification Number (EIN) with the IRS.

☐ File the appropriate tax election with the IRS such as the entity classification and "S" election.

☐ Contact the IRS for information on filing federal tax schedules.

☐ Obtain tax information such as record keeping requirements, facts about estimating taxes, etc.

☐ Investigate local business tax requirements such as reporting tangible personal property used to produce income on tax rendition forms.

☐ Investigate business insurance needs.

☐ Obtain the required city, county, or state business licenses and permits.

☐ If you have employees now or in the future, look into insurance or government requirements.

☐ Investigate/acquire Unemployment Insurance.

☐ Investigate/acquire Workers Comp.

☐ Investigate OSHA requirements.

☐ Investigate federal, state, and local tax information.

☐ Investigate self-employment tax.

☐ Investigate payroll taxes such as FICA, federal and state unemployment taxes.

☐ Get tax information on hiring independent contractors.

☐ Set up your business accounting system. Look into available small business accounting solution software packages.

☐ Register or reserve your Federal trademark/service mark and register appropriate copyrights.

☐ If marketing an invention, investigate patents.

☐ Order any required notices of intent to do business in the community.

☐ Identify communication equipment needs such as a business land line, cell phone, or PDA.

☐ Open a business bank account.

☐ Purchase office equipment and supplies.

☐ Order inventory, signage, and fixtures.

☐ Get email.

☐ Set up social media marketing accounts.

☐ Develop a website.

☐ Develop marketing materials, business cards, stationary, etc.

☐ Prepare sales literature.

☐ Explore financing options.

☐ Begin advertising campaign.

Appendix A

Feasibility Study

A Feasibility Study, or business opportunity analysis, is a planning tool similar to a business plan. The Feasibility Study is done to flesh out the possibilities of an initial business idea. The Business Plan then fully describes the business and its financial projections. The Feasibility Study represents a definition of a problem or opportunity to be studied, an analysis of the current mode of operation, a definition of the requirements, an evaluation of alternatives, and an agreed upon course of action. A Feasibility Study can be applied to any project.

Description of the Startup

Identification and exploration of business scenarios.

- List scenarios or business models of what the startup may look like, how it will be organized, and how it will generate profits.
- Eliminate the scenarios down to the best one or two.
- Flesh-out the scenario that appears to have the potential for further action.

Define the startup and alternative scenarios.

- Describe the type and quality of products or service (P/S) to be offered.
- Outline how the business will make money (i.e. the general business model).
- Describe the technical process including location, kind of inputs, etc.
- Specify the time-line from the time the startup begins until it is up and running at capacity.

Describe the relationship to the surrounding area.

- Give an outline of the economic and social impact on the community.
- Show the environmental impact on the surrounding area (if any).

Market Feasibility

Description of the Industry

- Describe the size and scope of the industry, market or market segments.
- Estimate the future direction of the industry, market or market segments.
- Describe the nature of the industry, market or market segments. Is it stable or changing and restructuring?
- Identify the life-cycle of the industry, market or market segments (emerging, growing, plateauing, mature, declining).

Industry Competitiveness

- Describe the industry concentration. Are there a few large or many small companies similar to your startup?
- Describe your competitors? Will you compete directly against them?
- What hindrances to startup businesses within your industry are there? Can new companies enter easily?
- What is the concentration and competitiveness of input suppliers?
- What is the concentration and competitiveness of customers?
- Describe the price competitiveness and price influencers of your product/service.

Market Potential

- Identify the demand and usage trends of your market or market segment.
- Examine the potential for new, niche, or segmented market opportunities.
- Assess your potential share of the market or market segment.

Access to Market Outlets

- Identify your customers and associated marketing costs.
- Investigate possible sales channels and the costs involved.

Sales Projection

- Estimate sales or service usage.
- Carefully identify and assess the accuracy of your assumptions (hypotheses) in the sales projection.
- Project sales under various assumptions (i.e. selling prices, services provided, etc.).

Technical Feasibility

Facility Needs.

- Estimate the size and type of facilities needed.
- Investigate the need for related buildings, equipment, vehicles, etc.

Suitability of Production Technology

- Investigate and compare technology providers.
- Determine reliability and competitiveness of technology (proven or unproven, state-of-the-art, etc.).
- Identify limitations or constraints of the technology.

Investigate Access to:

- Raw materials

- Transportation
- Labor

Raw Materials

- Estimate the amount of raw materials needed.
- Investigate the current and future availability and access to raw materials.
- Assess the quality and cost of raw materials.

Other inputs

- Investigate the availability of labor including wage rates, skill level, etc.
- Assess the potential to access and attract qualified management personnel.
- Analyze production inputs (electricity, natural gas, water, etc.)
- Investigate potential output problems (waste, emissions, etc.)
- Analyze other environmental impacts.
- Identify regulatory requirements.
- Explore economic development incentives.

Financial/Economic Feasibility

Estimate the total capital requirements

- Assess the "seed capital" needs of the business project during the investigation process and start-up, and how these needs will be met.
- Estimate capital requirements for facilities, equipment, and inventories.
- Estimate working capital needs.
- Estimate start-up capital needs until revenues are realized at full capacity.

- Estimate contingency capital needs due to construction delays, technology malfunction, market access delays, etc.
- Estimate other capital needs.

Estimate equity and credit needs

- Estimate equity needs.
- Identify alternative equity sources and capital availability (i.e. family, producers, local investors, angel investors, venture capitalists, etc.)
- Estimate credit needs.
- Identify and assess alternative credit sources - banks, government (i.e. direct loans or loan guarantees), grants and local and state economic development incentives.

Budget expected costs and returns of various alternatives

- Estimate the expected revenue, costs, profit margin and expected net profit.
- Estimate the sales or usage needed to break-even.
- Estimate the returns under various production, price and sales levels. This may involve identifying "best case," "typical," and "worst case" scenarios.
- Assess the reliability of the underlying assumptions of the analysis (prices, production, efficiencies, market access, market penetration, etc.)
- Benchmark against industry averages and competitors (cost, margin, profits, ROI, etc.).
- Identify limitations or constraints of the economic analysis.
- Calculate expected cash flows during the start-up period and when the business reaches capacity.
- Prepare pro forma income statement, balance sheet, and other statements of when the business is fully operating.

Organizational/Managerial Feasibility

Business Structure

- Identify the proposed legal structure of the business.
- Outline the staffing and governance structure of the business along with lines of authority and decision-making structure.
- Identify any potential joint venture partners, alliances or other important stakeholders.
- Identify the availability of skilled and experienced business managers.
- Identify the availability of consultants and service providers with the skills needed to realize the project, including legal, accounting, industry experts, etc.

Business Founders

- Character matters—are the people involved of outstanding character?
- Do the founders have the "fire in the belly" required to take the project to completion?
- Do the founders have the skills and ability to complete the project?
- What key individuals will lead the project?
- Is there a reward system for the founders? Is it based on business performance?
- Have the founders organized other successful businesses?

Study Conclusions

- Identify and describe alternative business scenarios and models.
- Compare and contrast scenarios based on goals of the producer group.
- Outline criteria for decision making among alternatives.

Next Step

After the feasibility study has been completed and presented to the leaders of the startup, they should carefully study and analyze the conclusions and underlying assumptions. Next, the leaders will be faced with deciding which course of action to pursue.

Potential courses of action include:

- Choosing the most viable business scenario or model, developing a business plan and proceeding with creating and operating a business.
- Identifying additional scenarios for further study.
- Deciding that a viable business opportunity is not available and moving to end the business investigation process.
- Following another course of action.

Appendix B

Sample Business Plan

Business plans come in many forms. There is not a particular business plan format better than another. Business plans are used within the company to keep the business on track and outside the company to present potential investors answer—in writing—to the questions they have regarding any business venture in which they may participate. The entrepreneur should do their research into the form and the content of business plans so that they will have the best document for their use and to present to investors. Some investors prefer brief but accurate information, other investors desire to see real numbers with charts and graphs.

Business Plan

Owners

- Business Name
- Address Line 1
- Address Line 2
- City, ST, ZIP Code
- Telephone
- Fax
- E-Mail

Executive Summary

- This section is a summary of the information from the pages that follow. Prepare it last, after the business plan has been written.
- The Executive Summary should not exceed two pages.
- Headings to use in the Executive Summary:
  - Vision/Mission Statement
  - Company Summary
  - Products/Services
  - Market Assessment
  - Strategic Implementation
  - Expected Outcomes

Vision/Mission Statement and Goals

- Vision Statement
  - Vision/mission statements are clear summaries of where the business is headed.
  - They describe what the business does and for whom.
  - They explain unique business characteristics.
  - They reflect the values of the company and the type of business culture being created.
- Goals and Objectives
  - What will your business achieve?
  - List specific terms of financial performance, resource commitments (time and money) and risk.
  - List milestones and when they will be achieved?
- Keys to Success
  - What you need or must happen, for the business to succeed?

Company Summary

The material in this section is an introduction to the company.

- Company Background
  - What does your business do?

- o Who were the founders?
- o What were the important milestones in developing the business?
- Resources, Facilities and Equipment
  - o What equipment is necessary for your products or services?
  - o What are the land, equipment, human and financial resources needed?
  - o Who provides them?
  - o How are providers and stakeholders rewarded?
- Marketing Methods
  - o Show your annual sales volume in dollars and units?
  - o Do you use forward contracting, options, or futures? If so, how?
  - o How much does it cost to produce and deliver your products and services?
  - o How is contracting used?
- Management and Organization
  - o Who is currently on the management team?
  - o How have management responsibilities been divided among the management team?
  - o What are the lines of authority?
  - o Who acts as the President/CEO? Spokesperson? Chief Financial Officer?
  - o Who determines employees' salaries and conducts performance reviews?
  - o What is the educational background of the management team members?
  - o What is the management team's reputation in the community?
  - o What special skills and abilities do the management team have?
  - o What additional skills does the management team need?
  - o Who are the key people and personnel that make your business run?

- o Who do you go to for advice and support?
- o Do management and employees have avenues for personal development?
- o Sketch a diagram of lines of authority for your operation.
- Ownership Structure
  - o Who are the primary stakeholders in your business?
  - o Describe the legal form of your company, such as partnership, proprietorship, or corporation.
  - o Do you need special permits to operate, or a record for inspections? If you do, please describe them.
- Social Responsibility
  - o What environmental practices do you follow?
  - o What procedures do you use for handling chemicals?
  - o What noise/dust/timing/odor policies do you have?
  - o What will be the roles of management and employees in community organizations?
  - o What will be your involvement at the local/state/national level in commodity organizations?
  - o What training and new employee orientation practices will you offer to insure proper handling of hazardous materials and safe operation of equipment?
- Internal Analysis
  - o What are the strengths and weaknesses of your firm?
  - o What are the relative strengths of each enterprise or business unit within the firm?
  - o What are the core competencies (things you are doing better than others) of your firm?
  - o What things can you build on? Think only about the things that you can control.
  - o Suggested areas to consider:
    - knowledge and work
    - financial position
    - productivity

- family
- lifestyle
- location
- resources
  - What enterprise or business unit should be exited?
  - What enterprise or business unit shows promise?

Products and Services

- Describe the products and services you plan to sell.
- How is your product or service unique?
- Are you producing a commodity or a differentiated product?
- How does your product or service compare to other products in quality, price, and location?
- What experience do you have with this product/service?

Market Assessment

- Examining the General Market
  - How is the market characterized?
  - Are there clear segments in the market? Describe them.
  - What important customer need(s) is the market not currently fulfilling?
  - What is the growth potential for each segment of the market?
  - What opportunities and threats does your firm face?
  - Who is your competition?
  - What trends, relevant to your business, do you see?
  - What political and legal issues do you face, such as zoning, environmental laws, inspections, etc.?
- Customer Analysis
  - Who will be your customers?
  - What do you sell to each of the customers?
  - How does your product/service solve a key customer problem?
  - How difficult is it to retain a customer?

o How much does it cost to support a customer?
- Industry Analysis
- Strategic Alternatives

Strategic Implementation

- Production
    o How will you produce your product?
    o What value will you create and capture with your product?
    o What is your competitive advantage?
    o What technology will you use, i.e. reduced tillage, GPS systems, etc.?
    o What processes will you use to produce products?
    o What growth options will you use to develop the business unit?
    o What is the anticipated timeline?
- Resource Needs
    o To effectively organize your business you need to insure the resources are available. Assess those needs here.
        ▪ Human
        ▪ What skills are needed?
        ▪ How will human resources be acquired?
        ▪ Financial
        ▪ What level of financial resources will be needed?
        ▪ Physical
        ▪ What type, quantity and quality of physical resources will be required?
- Sourcing/Procurement Strategy
    o On what do you base a decision to buy products or services? Price? Quality? Convenience? Extra service? A combination?
    o By what venue will you find suppliers — local dealer, internet, direct from the manufacturer, etc.?
- Marketing Strategy

- o What is your sales plan?
- o What advertising and promotion will be used to increase sales/awareness?
- o Where will you sell products/services?
- o Will you use the open market or contracts?
- o Do you have a preferred market outlet?
- o Are you a qualified supplier for a specific processor or buyer?
- o How will you price the product?
    - Hedging, forward pricing, options
- o How will you use these to mitigate your risk?
- o Will you use production or marketing contracting to reduce risk?
- Performance Standards
    - o What performance standards will be used to monitor this enterprise or business unit?
    - o What are acceptable performance standards?
    - o What yield or output levels could you attain?
    - o What efficiency levels will you reach?
    - o What procedures will be used to monitor performance?
    - o Who is responsible for monitoring performance?
    - o What industry benchmarks will be used to assess performance?

Financial Plan

- Financial Projections
    - o How will you fund the business?
    - o What are your desired debt and equity position?
    - o Who will provide capital debt funds?
    - o What role will leasing play in your financial strategy?
    - o Will you use outside investors for equity capital?
    - o How will you manage the financial risks your business faces?

- o What operating procedures, such as developing cash flow budgets or spending limits, will you have to ensure adequate money for debt repayment?
- o What are the important assumptions that underlie your projections? These assumptions may be associated with both external and internal factors.
- o What financial aspects of your business (equity, asset growth, ROA, ROE, etc.) will you monitor?
- o What procedures will be used for monitoring overall business performance?
- o What level of performance will your business target? These should be targets for next year and in five years. They should be financial performance standards used to monitor the overall business.
- o What yield and output levels could you attain? What efficiency levels will you reach?
- Contingency Plan
  - o What will you do if you can't follow through with your primary plan?
  - o How are you preparing for an emergency in your business?
  - o How will the business function if something happens to one of the key members of the management team?

Appendix C

Business & Money Making Ideas

- Creative Ideas
  - Sell Arts and Crafts
  - Interior Design
  - Make and Sale Jewelry
- Do What You Love
  - Freelance Your Experience
  - Monetize Your Hobby
  - Photography/Graphic Design
- Product Sales
  - Open a Store and Sale Merchandise
  - Direct Sale (Amway, Herbalife, etc.)
  - Sale Online (eBay or Etsy)
  - Open an Internet Store (Shopify)
  - Sale Gift Baskets
  - Swap Meets or Flea Market Sales
  - Open a Thrift Store
  - Sale at a Flea Market
- B to B
  - Bookkeeping
  - Business Support
  - Consulting
  - Desktop Publishing
  - Security Specialist

- Social Media Specialist
- Video Recording
- Virtual Assistance
- Personal Services
  - Child Care
  - Elder Care
  - Financial Advisor
  - Organizer
  - Personal Concierge
  - Personal Shopper
  - Remodeling Designer/Contractor
  - Tutoring
  - Wedding Consultant
  - Lawn Care
  - Cleaning
  - Catering
  - Event Planning
  - Answering Services

Senior Care Businesses

- Senior Day Care Centre
- Elder Transitional Living
- Elder Home Assistance
- Elder Concierge Service
  - Support
  - Administrative Assistance
  - Personal Errands

- o Shopping
- o Fitness Assistance
- o Computer Training Assistance
- o Pet Care
- o Meal Prep
- Elder Transportation

Pet Businesses

- Pooper Scooper (clean up)
- Pet Photography
- Pet Clothing, Accessories, and Toys
- Pet Sitting
- Pet Day Care Service
- Obedience Training
- Dog Walking
- Aquarium Cleaning
- Gourmet Pet Treats

Part-Time Businesses

- Antique Picking
- Computer Tutor
- Custom Jewelry
- Garage/Attic Cleaning
- Handyman
- Medical Transcription
- Window Tinting
- Office and Home Organizer
- Personal Chef

- Personal Trainer
- Picture Framer
- Maintenance
- Records Search
- Food Delivery
- T-shirt Designer
- Yoga Instructor
- Mobile Bet Grooming
- Diaper Delivery
- Dry Cleaning Pickup/Delivery
- Mobile Locksmith
- Graffiti Removal
- Self-Defense Instructor
- Adventure Tours
- Mobile Massage Therapy
- Mobile Mechanic/Oil Changing
- Seamstress/Tailor
- Court-paper Service
- Resume Service
- Mystery Shopping
- Tax Form Preparer
- Wedding Guide Publishing
- Mobile Car Washing
- Used-Car Inspection
- Power Washing
- Private Investigation

- Planner/Business Consulting
- Packing/Unpacking Service
- Travel Management
- Carpet Cleaning/Dying
- Hospital Bill Auditing
- Specialized Staffing
- Computer Repair
- Referral Service
- Long-distance Reselling
- Computer Consulting
- Limousine Service
- Language Translator
- Proof-reading/Editing
- Office Consultant
- Mini-Blind Cleaning/Window Washing
- Apartment Prepping
- Debt Collections
- Seminar Promotions
- Valet Parking
- Sales-Lead Generating
- Public Relations Agency
- Direct Mailing
- Mailing Services
- Sales Training
- Welcoming Services
- Pool Servicing

- Lawn Care
- Home Inspection Service
- House Painting
- Local Moving Services
- House Sitting
- Home Decorating
- Party Planning
- Child Identification Program
- Child Transportation Services
- Baby-proofing
- Nanny Services
- Home Infant Care
- Video Historiography
- Video Taping Services
- Reunion Organizing
- Home Cleaning with Allergy-Free Products
- Christmas Decorating/Light Installation
- House Staging
- Teach Handyman Skills

Appendix D

Entrepreneurship Glossary

- **Accelerator (Seed Accelerator or Startup Accelerator):** Fixed-term, cohort-based programs, that include mentorship and educational components and culminate in a public pitch event or demo day. While traditional business incubators are often government-funded, generally take no equity, and focus on biotech, medical technology, clean tech or product-centric companies, accelerators can be either privately or publicly funded and focus on a wide range of industries. Unlike business incubators, the application process for seed accelerators is open to anyone, but highly competitive. There are specific types of seed accelerators, such as corporate accelerators, which are often subsidiaries or programs of larger corporations that act like seed accelerators.

- **Accountant:** See Certified Public Accountant

- **Accounts Receivable:** The money owed to the business after goods or services have been provided. The sum of all customer accounts receivable are listed as current assets on the balance sheet.

- **Accounts Payable:** All bills to vendors that has not yet been paid. The sum of all accounts payable are listed as current liability on the balance sheet.

- **Adaptation:** Modification of a concept or object to make it applicable in situations different from originally anticipated. As a business enters a new market, it must cope with cultural and demographic differences in the way it handles marketing. Some businesses choose a standardization model, in which the business appeals to universal needs, wants or goals in its marketing. An alternative, the adaptation marketing strategy, forgoes universality in favor of tailoring marketing to appeal to the cultural or demographic particulars of customers in the new market.

- **Advertising:** The act or practice of calling public attention to one's product, service, need, etc., especially by paid announcements in newspapers and magazines, over radio or television, on billboards, etc.

- **AdWords Campaign:** An AdWords Campaign is an ad campaign within an AdWords account. An AdWords campaign is usually composed of several ad groups. Each ad group serves different ad texts based on the type of keyword a user may type into Google's search engine.

- **Angel Investors (Angel):** Individuals who have capital that they are willing to risk. Angels are often successful entrepreneurs who invest in emerging entrepreneurial ventures, often as a bridge from the self-funded stage to the point in which a business can attract venture capital. See Super-angel investor

- **Angel Network:** A group of angel investors who have organized to invest collectively, operate more effectively and provide mutual support. Also known as angel groups

- **Ansoff Matrix:** A strategic planning tool that provides a framework to help executives, senior managers, and marketers devise strategies for future growth. It is named after Russian American Igor Ansoff, who came up with the concept.

- **Autoresponder:** A program that automatically generates a set response to all messages sent to a particular e-mail address. (i.e. Mailchimp, Traffic Wave, Awebber, Get Response, etc.)

- **Asset Earning Power:** A common performance measure in corporate finance, used to determine a firm's efficiency in generating earnings from its asset base. Asset earning power is calculated as: Asset Earning Power = Earnings Before Taxes (EBT)/Total Assets.

- **Asset Turnover Ratio:** The ratio of the value of a

company's sales or revenues generated relative to the value of its assets. The Asset Turnover ratio can often be used as an indicator of the efficiency with which a company is deploying its assets in generating revenue.

- **Assets**: Items of value owned by a company and shown on the balance sheet, including cash, equipment, inventory, etc.

- **B to B**: On the Internet, B2B (business-to-business), also known as e-biz, is the exchange of products, services or information (aka e-commerce) between businesses, rather than between businesses and consumers.

- **B to C**: Business to consumer (B2C) is business or transactions conducted directly between a company and consumers who are the end-users of its products or services. While most companies that sell directly to consumers can be referred to as B2C companies, the term became immensely popular during the dotcom boom of the late 1990s, when it was used mainly to refer to online retailers, as well as other companies that sold products and services to consumers through the internet.

- **Balance Sheet**: Summary statement of a company's financial position at a given point in time, listing assets as well as liabilities.

- **Bankruptcy**: A legal proceeding involving a person or business that is unable to repay outstanding debts. The bankruptcy proceedings begin with a petition filed by the debtor, which is most common, or on the behalf of creditors. It is a generalized term for a federal court procedure that helps people and business owners get rid of their debts and repay their creditors.

- **Bookkeeping**: The activity or occupation of keeping records of the financial affairs of a business.
  - A **single-entry bookkeeping system** or single-entry accounting system is a method of bookkeeping relying on a one-sided accounting entry to maintain

financial information.

- o The **double entry system of accounting** or bookkeeping means that every business transaction will involve two accounts (or more). For example, when a company borrows money from its bank, the company's Cash account will increase and its liability account Loans Payable will increase.

- **Bootstrapping:** A situation in which an entrepreneur starts a company with little capital. An individual is said to be boot strapping when he or she attempts to found and build a company from personal finances or from the operating revenues of the new company.

- **Bottom Line:** The final total of an account, balance sheet, or another financial document.

- **Branding:** The marketing practice of creating a name, symbol or design that identifies and differentiates a product from other products. An effective brand strategy gives you a major edge in increasingly competitive markets.

- **Breakeven Point**: Dollar value of sales that will cover, but not exceed, all of the company's costs, both fixed and variable.

- **Bridge Finance:** Short-term finance that is expected to be repaid quickly.

- **Build/Measure/Learn:** A core component of Lean Startup methodology is the build-measure-learn feedback loop. The first step is figuring out the problem that needs to be solved and then developing a minimum viable product (MVP) to begin the process of learning as quickly as possible.

- **Burn Rate:** The speed per month at which your startup capital is being used up before you are able to have a positive cash flow.

- **Business Incubator:** This is a form of mentoring in which workspace, coaching, and support services are provided to entrepreneurs and early-stage businesses at a free or reduced cost.

- **Business Cycle:** The fluctuation in economic activity that an economy experiences over a period of time; basically defined in terms of periods of expansion or recession.

- **Business Model:** How and where you run your company is your business model. A franchise is one business model. An online store, home goods retailer and home-based business are other models. How you deliver your product or service to customers also defines your business model. Shipping goods directly to your customers is one delivery method. Shipping your goods from a warehouse is another common delivery mode. It identifies the services that your customers value and shows the reciprocation of funds for the services your small business renders to your customers. Of course, your small business may have more than one method of generating income. Still, the business model simplifies the money process by focusing on the largest income generator.

- **Business Plan:** A written document detailing a proposed venture, covering current status, expected needs, and projected results for the enterprise. It contains a thorough analysis of the product or service being offered, the market and competition, the marketing strategy, the operating plan, and the management as well as profit, balance sheet, and cash flow projections. →The business plan provides the details of your business. It takes the focus of the *business model* and builds upon it. It explains the equipment and staff needed to meet the details of the business model. It also explains the marketing strategy of your small business, or how your business will attract and retain customers, and deal with the competition. →Furthermore, the business plan explains the financial stability of your small business at a particular point in time, as well as in the forecasted future. Overall, the business plan supports the business model and explains the steps needed to achieve the goals of that model.

- **Business Plan vis-à-vis Business Model:** The business plan is completely dependent upon the business model. The *business model* explains the flow of money within the company and the *business plan* explains the structure needed to obtain that flow of money. If you change the business model, you will also need to change the business plan.

- **Capital:** Cash or goods used to generate income. For entrepreneurs, capital often refers to the funds and other assets invested in the business venture.

- **Capital Expenditure:** Money spent by a business or organization on acquiring or maintaining fixed assets, such as land, buildings, and equipment.

- **Capital Injection:** An investment of capital generally in the form of cash or equity—and rarely assets—into a business or company.

- **Cash Flow:** The difference between the company's cash receipts and its cash payments in a given period. It refers to the amount of money actually available to make purchases and pay current bills and obligations.

- **Cash Flow Statement:** A summary of a company's cash flow over a period of time.

- **Certified Public Accountant (CPA):** An accounting professional who has passed the Uniform CPA examination and has also met additional state certification and experience requirements.

- **Client Retention:** The practice that a business engages in to retain their customer base after the sale has been made; e.g. customer service.

- **Coach:** A qualified coach is the person hired to help keep the entrepreneur on track and on target. They are not the same as an advisor or mentor.

- **Collateral:** An asset pledged as security for a loan.

- **Commercialization:** The process of introducing a new product or production method into commerce—making it available on the market.

- **Copyright:** Copyright is a form of legal protection for published and unpublished literary, scientific, and artistic works that have been fixed in a tangible or material form. It grants exclusive rights to the work's creator for a specified period of time.

- **Core Competencies of Marketing:** The ability to identify with the wants and needs of the target customer and communicate the company's brand image and product value in such a way as to elicit a favorable reaction from that target customer. →Innovation expertise, speed and flexibility in the marketplace, superior product development skills, greater marketplace and customer understanding, strong analysis and database skills, industry/market knowledge and expertise, experts in marketing communications, fast or friendly customer service, streamlined and efficient processes, logistics expertise, strategic/entrepreneurial insight, skills in the early identification of trends/opportunities, trend identification, strategic planning, message creation and effective communication in written and graphic form are some examples of core competencies.

- **Corporate Tax:** A corporate tax is a levy placed on the profit of a firm to raise taxes. After operating earnings is calculated by deducting expenses including the cost of goods sold (COGS) and depreciation from revenues, enacted tax rates are applied to generate a legal obligation the business owes the government.

- **Corporation:** A business form that is an entity legally separate from its owners. Its important features include limited liability, easy transfer of ownership, and unlimited life.

- **Cost Benefit Analysis (CBA):** A process by which business decisions are analyzed where the benefits of a given situation or business actions are summed, and then the costs associated with taking that action are subtracted.

- **Cost of Capital:** This is the true cost of securing the funds that the business uses to pay for its asset base. Some funds are from debt (less risky to the creditors, so it has a lower cost of capital to the firm), and some funds come from equity (riskier to the investors, so these have a higher cost of capital). The combination of lower-cost debt capital with higher-cost equity capital produces the next item in this list.

- **Cost of Goods Sold (CGS):** The direct costs attributable to the production of the goods sold by a company. This amount includes the cost of the materials used in creating the good along with the direct labour costs used to produce the good. *CGS* measures the expense a company incurs in procuring the item to sell, and the *sales revenue* measures the money brought in by selling the product. From these two figures, you can calculate the *gross margin* as well as the *gross margin percentage*. The higher your company's gross margin percentage, the more profit you make for each dollar of sales. However, the gross margin does not account for overhead or taxes, so it is not the only metric to consider.

- **Cottage Industry:** a business or manufacturing activity carried on in a person's home. See home-based business

- **Credit:** A credit is an accounting entry that either increases a liability or equity account, or decreases an asset or expense account.

- **Crowdfunding (crowdsourcing):** The practice of funding a project or venture by raising many small amounts of money from a large number of people, typically via the Internet.

- **Customer Development:** A process developed by serial entrepreneur Steve Blank, customer development is the practice of gaining customer insights to generate, test, and optimize ideas for products and services through interviews and structured experiments.

- **DBA:** Abbreviation for Doing Business As that refers to the trade name used by the company to conduct or promote a business.

- **Debit:** A debit is an accounting entry that either increases an asset or expense account, or decreases a liability or equity account. It is positioned to the left in an accounting entry.

- **Deductions:** Expenditures for business items that have no future life (such as rent, utilities or wages) and are incurred in conducting normal business activities which a business owner may deduct from gross earned income for federal tax purposes.

- **Depreciation:** The decrease in the value of assets over their expected life by an accepted accounting method, such as allocating the cost of an asset over the years in which it is used.

- **Discounted Cash Flow (DCF):** A valuation method used to estimate the attractiveness of an investment opportunity. DCF analysis uses future cash flow projections and discounts them to arrive at a present value estimate, which is used to evaluate the potential for investment. If the value arrived at through DCF analysis is higher than the current cost of the investment, the opportunity may be a good one.

- **Direct Sales:** Direct selling is the marketing and selling of products directly to consumers away from a fixed retail location. Peddling is the oldest form of direct selling. Modern direct selling includes sales made through the party plan, one-on-one demonstrations, and other personal contact arrangements as well as internet sales. The top ten direct sales companies are Amway, Avon, Herbalife, Mary Kay, Vorwerk, Natura, Infinitus,

Tupperware, Nu Skin Enterprises, and JoyMain (2015).

- **Double Loop Learning:** Chris Argyris (1976) proposes double loop learning theory which pertains to learning to change underlying values and assumptions. The focus of the theory is on solving problems that are complex and ill-structured and which change as problem-solving advances.

- **Economic Bubble:** An economic cycle determined by rapid escalation of asset prices followed by a contraction of the value of the asset. It is created by a surge in asset prices unwarranted by the fundamentals of the asset and driven by exuberant market behavior.

- **E-commerce:** The sale of products and services over the Internet.

- **Ecosystem:** See Entrepreneurial Ecosystem

- **Entrepreneur:** A person who organizes, operates, and assumes the risk for a business venture.

- **Entrepreneurial Ecosystem**: refers to the elements – individuals, organizations or institutions – outside the individual entrepreneur that are conducive to, or inhibitive of, the choice of a person to become an entrepreneur, or the probabilities of his or her success following launch.

- **Equity:** An ownership interest in a business. [Equity is money obtained from the investors in exchange for ownership of a company, while debt is bank loans etc. that must be paid back.]

- **Executive Summary:** or management summary, is a short document or section of a document, produced for business purposes, that summarizes a longer report or proposal or a group of related reports in such a way that readers can rapidly become acquainted with a large body of material without having to read it all.

- **Exit Strategy:** A contingency plan that is executed by an investor, trader, venture capitalist or business owner to liquidate their investment in the business or to dispose of tangible business assets once certain predetermined criteria for either has been met or executed.

- **Feasibility Study:** An analysis and evaluation of a proposed project to determine if it (1) is technically feasible, (2) is feasible within the estimated cost, and (3) will be profitable. Feasibility studies are almost always conducted where large sums are at stake. Also called feasibility analysis. See also cost benefit analysis (CBA)

- **Financial Leverage:** The use of debt to acquire additional assets. Financial leverage is also known as trading on equity. Example: Bob uses $400,000 of his cash to purchase 40 acres of land with a total cost of $400,000. Sue uses $400,000 of her cash and borrows $800,000 to purchase 120 acres of land having a total cost of $1,200,000. Sue is using financial leverage. Sue is controlling $1,200,000 of land with only $400,000 of her own money.

- **Fixed Asset Base:** This is the long-term base of the company's operation strategy, represented by all the equipment, machinery, vehicles, facilities, IT infrastructure and long-term contracts the firm has invested in to conduct business. From a finance perspective, these assets are the revenue generators. When the entrepreneur decides to invest in a certain fixed asset configuration, that becomes the base from which the company functions week in and week out, doing business and servicing its customers.

- **Fixed Costs:** Business costs, such as rent, that are constant whatever the quantity of goods or services produced. See also variable costs

- **Flow Through Taxation:** A flow-through entity (FTE) is a legal entity where income "flows through" to investors or owners; that is, the income of the entity is treated as the income of the investors or owners. Flow-through entities are also known as pass-through entities or fiscally-transparent entities.

- **Funding Gap:** The amount of money needed to fund the ongoing operations or future development of a business or project that is not currently provided by cash, equity, or debt. Funding gaps can be overcome by investment from venture capital or angel investors, equity sales, or through debt offerings ad bank loans.

- **General Manager:** Serves as the top executive for the company and is responsible for strategy, structure, budgets, people and financial outcomes.

- **Gross Domestic Product (GDP):** The total value of goods produced and services provided in a country annually. The GDP is one of the primary indicators used to gauge the health of a country's economy. It represents the total dollar value of all goods and services produced over a specified time period.

- **Gross Income:** An intermediate earnings figure before all expenses are included, and net income is the final amount of profit or loss after all expenses are included.

- **Gross Margin:** The difference between revenue and cost of goods sold (COGS) divided by revenue, expressed as a percentage. Generally, it is calculated as the selling price of an item, less the cost of goods sold (production or acquisition costs, essentially).

- **Home-based Business:** A business, of any size or type, whose primary office is in the owner's home. See cottage industry

- **Income Statement:** Also known as a **"profit and loss statement**," it shows a firm's income and expenses, and the resulting profit or loss over a specified period of time.

- **Industry:** A classification that refers to groups of companies that are related based on their primary business activities. Describes a much more specific grouping of companies with highly similar business activities. Essentially, industries are created by further breaking down sectors into more defined groupings. Each of the dozen or so sectors will have a varying number of industries, but it can be in the hundreds. For example, the financial sector can be broken down into industries such as asset management, life insurance and Northwest regional banks. The Northwest regional bank industry, which is part of the financial sector, will only contain companies that operate banks in the Northwestern states. See also sector

- **Incubator (Business Incubator):** An organization designed to accelerate the growth and success of entrepreneurial companies through an array of business support resources and services that could include physical space, capital, coaching, common services, and networking connections.

- **Innovation:** The process of translating an idea or invention into a good or service that creates value or for which customers will pay. [Innovation = Invention + Commercialization]

- **Inputs:** Resources such as people, raw materials, energy, information, or finance that are put into a business to obtain a desired output. Inputs are classified under costs in accounting. When calculating the cost of goods sold for a particular item it is important to include not only the direct inputs such as raw materials but also indirect costs such as labor and overhead.

- **Intangible Assets:** Items of value that have no tangible physical properties, such as ideas.

- **Intellectual Property (assets):** The knowledge, experience, and skills that have been obtained, persevered, catalogued and made available for sharing.

- **Iteration:** The act of repeating a process with the aim of approaching a desired goal, target or result. Each repetition of the process is also called an "iteration", and the results of one iteration are used as the starting point for the next iteration. A product or process often goes through many iterations before it becomes profitable.

- **Internal Rate of Return (IRR):** Every decision enacted by the entrepreneur must be viewed in terms of its internally generated return to the company. Unlike the simple division used to find the ROI, the IRR compares the net expected returns over the useful life of a project being reviewed by management to the funds spent on that decision (or project). All projects must meet a certain IRR in order to be acceptable for investment by the company. If a project cannot meet a minimum IRR, then don't invest in it.
- **Intrepreneur:** A person who behaves like an entrepreneur whilst being employed. Intrepreneurs are usually encouraged to develop their ideas into a workable product by the companies for whom they work. Like an entrepreneur, an intrepreneur is motivated, creative, and able to think outside of the box.
- **Inventory:** Finished goods, work in process of manufacture, and raw materials owned by a company.
- **Investment Turnover Ratio:** The annual net sales to the total assets.
- **Joint venture:** A legal entity created by two or more businesses joining together to conduct a specific business enterprise with both parties sharing profits and losses.
- **Kirton Adapation-Innovation Theory:** The Adaption Innovation Theory is founded on the assumption that all people solve problems and are creative. The theory sharply distinguishes between level and style of creativity, problem solving and decision making and is concerned only with style. Both potential and evident capacity aside the theory states that people are different in cognitive style in which they are creative, solve problems and make decisions. These style differences lie on a normally

distributed continuum, ranging from high adaption to high innovation. The key to the distinction is that the more adaptive prefer their problems to be associated with more structure and more of this structure to be consensually agreed than do the more innovative. The more innovative are comfortable solving problems with less structure and are less concerned that the structure be consensually agreed than are the more adaptive.

- **Lead (Lead Generation):** Lead generation, in marketing, is the initiation of consumer interest or inquiry into products or services of a business. Leads can be created for purposes such as list building, e-newsletter list acquisition or for sales. A lead can also be a potential sales contact or a person that expresses interest in goods or services. Often leads are gained through the referral of an existing customer or through direct response to advertising.

- **Learning Organization:** The business term given to a company that facilitates the learning of its members and continuously transforms itself. The concept was coined through the work and research of Peter Senge and his colleagues.

- **Leverage:** See financial leverage

- **Liabilities:** Debts a business owes, including accounts payable, taxes, bank loans, and other obligations. Short-term liabilities are due within a year, while long-term liabilities are due in a period of time greater than a year.

- **Lean Startup:** An approach to business development that is based on the principles of lean production, a manufacturing methodology that values a business' ability to change quickly.

- **Leasehold Improvements**: The enhancements paid for by a tenant to leased space. Examples of leasehold improvements are: Interior walls and ceilings.

- **Limited Partnership:** A business arrangement in which the day-to-day operations are controlled by one or more general partners and funded by limited or silent partners who are legally responsible for losses based on the amount of their investment.

- **Line of Credit:** (1) An arrangement between a bank and a customer specifying the maximum amount of unsecured debt the customer can owe the bank at a given point in time. (2) A limit set by a seller on the amount that a purchaser can buy on credit.

- **Liquidity:** The ability of an asset to be converted to cash as quickly as possible and without any price discount.

- **Market Concentration:** A function of the number of companies and their respective shares of the total production (alternatively, total capacity or total reserves) in a market. Alternative terms are Industry concentration and Seller concentration.

- **Market Segmentation:** see segmentation

- **Marketable Outputs:** Marketable outputs includes finished products, finished goods (parts), and services. See Outputs

- **Marketing:** The process of researching, promoting, selling, and distributing a product or service. Marketing covers a broad range of practices, including advertising, publicity, promotion, pricing, and packaging.

- **Marketing Mix:** A combination of factors that can be controlled by a company to influence consumers to purchase its products.

- **Marketing Plan:** A document describing a firm's potential customers and a comprehensive strategy to sell them goods and services

- **Mentor:** A person who is willing to be a sounding board for your ideas, provides guidance, teaches or directs you to the needed resources and is willing to tell you what you need to hear and not what you want to hear.

- **Merger:** The joining together of two previously separate corporations. In the legal sense, two corporations dissolve and form a new entity with combined assets.

- **Minimum Viable Product (MVP):** A Lean Startup Term meaning the product which has just enough features to gather validated learning about the product and its development.

- **Networking:** (1) Developing business contacts to form business relationships, increase knowledge, expand a business, or serve the community. (2) Linking computers systems together.

- **Net Income (NI):** A company's total earnings (or profit). Net income is calculated by taking revenues and adjusting for the cost of doing business, depreciation, interest, taxes and other expenses.

- **Niche Marketing:** Identifying and targeting markets not adequately served by competitors.

- **Non-systematic risk:** The risks that are entirely unique to your company, products, buyers, promotional programs, billing, pricing, IT system and so on are non-systematic risks specific to your firm. Although there's little you can do to avoid or mitigate exposure to systematic risk, it is possible to use various diversification strategies to offset risks that are unique to your business. When working with risk premium, systematic risk and non-systematic risk, the rule is that the expected return on the business operations will always be directly related to the amount of risk taken on: Lower risk decisions come with lower expected returns, and higher risk decisions come with higher expected returns.

- **Occupational Safety and Health Administration (OSHA):** With the Occupational Safety and Health Act of 1970, Congress created the Occupational Safety and Health Administration (OSHA) to assure safe and healthful working conditions for working men and women by setting and enforcing standards and by providing training, outreach, education and assistance.

- **Operating Costs:** The expenses which are related to the operation of a business, or to the operation of a device, component, piece of equipment or facility. They are the cost of resources used by an organization just to maintain its existence. An easy way to determine the operating expenses for a particular business is to think about the costs that are eliminated by shutting down production for a period of time. When production costs stop, the operating costs (lease payments, utilities, insurance, etc.) remain.

- **Organizational Behavior (OB):** Studies the impact individuals, groups, and structures have on human behavior within organizations. It is an interdisciplinary field that includes sociology, psychology, communication, and management.

- **Organizational Development (OD):** A field of research, theory, and practice dedicated to expanding the knowledge and effectiveness of people to accomplish more successful organizational change and performance.

- **Organizational Ethics:** Organizational ethics are the principals and standards by which businesses operate, according to Reference for Business. They are best demonstrated through acts of fairness, compassion, integrity, honor and responsibility

- **Organizational Values:** Every organization has a set of values, whether or not they are written down. The values guide the perspective of the organization as well as its actions. Writing down a set of commonly-held values can help an organization define its culture and beliefs.

- **Outputs:** Everything that is generated as a result of the company being in business such as: products (services), waste, contaminated air or water, heat, economic wealth to the employees, community, shareholders, etc. See Marketable Outputs

- **Outsourcing:** The practice of using subcontractors or other businesses, rather than paid employees, for standard services such as accounting, payroll, information technology, advertising, etc.

- **Overhead Expenses:** A cost that does not vary with the level of production or sales, and usually a cost not directly involved with production or sales. The costs that are more static and relate to general business functions, such as paying accounting personnel and facility costs. Overhead expenses are administrative expenses such as salaries, rent, utility bills, insurance, travel expenses, benefits to employees. Overhead costs are usually more constant in their value, while operating expenses tend to fluctuate depending on the product or service that the company provides.

- **Partnership:** Legal form of business in which two or more persons are co-owners, sharing profits and losses. Patent: A property right granted to an inventor to exclude others from making, using, offering for sale, or selling an invention for a limited time in exchange for public disclosure of the invention when the patent is granted.

- **Pivot:** "Pivoting" is a familiar word in the startup world. When your first business model isn't working (and this happens more often than not), the CEO and team pivot to plan-B. Eric Ries, the creator of the 'Lean Startup' methodology, reminds us that pivots imply keeping one foot firmly in place as you shift the other in a new direction. In this way, new ventures process what they have already learned from past success and failure and apply these insights in new areas.

- **Product Development:** A strategy employed when a company's existing market is saturated, and revenues and profits are stagnant or falling. There is little or no opportunity for growth. A product development diversification strategy takes a company outside its existing business and a new product is developed for a new market. An example of this strategy is a company that has sold insurance products and decides to develop a financial education program aimed at college students. The new product is not revolutionary as there are other companies producing similar products, but it is new to the company producing it.

- **Production Cost:** The direct materials, direct labor, and manufacturing overhead used to manufacture products. The production costs are also referred to as manufacturing costs, product costs, a manufacturer's inventoriable costs, or the costs occurring in the factory.

- **Profitability Ratios**: A class of financial metrics that are used to assess a business's ability to generate earnings as compared to its expenses and other relevant costs incurred during a specific period of time. For most of these ratios, having a higher value relative to a competitor's ratio or the same ratio from a previous period is indicative that the company is doing well.

- **Pro-forma Financial Statement:** A statement based on certain assumptions and projections. For example, a corporation might want to see the effects of three different financing options. Therefore, it prepares projected balance sheets, income statements, and statements of cash flows

- **Purchase Order (PO):** A commercial document and first official offer issued by a buyer to a seller, indicating types, quantities, and agreed prices for products or services.

- **Ratio Analysis:** A form of Financial Statement Analysis that is used to obtain a quick indication of a firm's financial performance in several key areas. The ratios are categorized as Short-term Solvency Ratios, Debt Management Ratios, Asset Management Ratios, Profitability Ratios, and Market Value Ratios.

- **Return on Investment (ROI):** The only way to think about your business is with an ROI perspective. The entrepreneur has committed capital investment into a certain combination of assets, from which the company generates sales. Those sales cover the costs of operations and hopefully produce a profit. That profit, divided by the total funds invested in the company (the assets), equals the ROI to the entrepreneur. Think of it this way: Would you work all those hours and take on all that responsibility if your ROI was only 6 percent annually? The stronger the profit picture compared to the total funds employed in the enterprise, the higher the ROI.

- **Revenue:** Income, especially of a company or organization and of a substantial nature.

- **Risk Premium:** Entrepreneurs must understand that every decision they consider has an inherent level of risk associated with it. If project A is far riskier than project B, there should be a clear risk premium that could accrue to the firm if project A is enacted. But with that risk premium return, there will also be a risk premium cost to the company for the use of the funds. Business owners always have to decide whether the risk premium of additional potential return is commensurate with the additional risk costs that come with doing that investment project.

- **Sales Channel(s):** A way or ways of bringing products or services to market so that they can be purchased by consumers. A sales channel can be direct if it involves a business selling directly to its customers, or it can be indirect if an intermediary such as a retailer or dealer is involved in selling the product to customers. The methods used to exchange goods or services with money.

- **Sales Metrics:** The variables used to define how you will achieve your sales projections.

- **Sales Records:** The information you have on your customers, including but not limited to their contact information, how often they purchase from you, what they purchase and how they pay their bills. Your company's sales records are quite likely to prove your most valuable marketing information source.

- **Scalable Business:** An analogous meaning is implied when the word is used in an economic context, where scalability of a company implies that the underlying business model offers the potential for economic growth within the company. Scalability refers to the ability of a site to increase in size as demand warrants.

- **Sector:** One of a few general segments in the economy within which a large group of companies can be categorized. An economy can be broken down into about a dozen sectors, which can describe nearly all of the business activity in that economy. For example, the basic materials sector is the segment of the economy in which companies deal in the business of exploration, processing and selling the basic materials such as gold, silver or aluminum which are used by other sectors of the economy. →The terms industry and sector are often used interchangeably to describe a group of companies that operate in the same segment of the economy or share a similar business type. Although the terms are commonly used interchangeably, they do, in fact, have slightly different meanings. This difference pertains to their scope; a sector refers to a large segment of the economy, while the term industry describes a much more specific group of companies or businesses.

- **Seed financing:** A relatively small amount of money provided to prove a concept; it may involve product development and market research.

- **Segmentation (Market Segmentation):** Demographic segmentation is market segmentation according to locations, age, race, religion, gender, family size, ethnicity, income, and education. Demographics can be segmented into several markets to help an organization target its consumers more accurately.

- **Segmented Addressable Market (SAM):** Or Served Available Market is the portion of the total available market that will be targeted. The SAM is the portion of the market whom your current business model is targeting. See Share of Available Market, Total Available Market, and segmentation.
- **Service Core of Retired Executives (SCORE):** A non-profit organization dedicated to entrepreneurs' education and the success of small business. It is sponsored by the SBA to provide consulting to small businesses.
- **Share of the Market (SOM):** The share of the market or the subset of the SAM that you will realistically reach. The SOM is the portion of the SAM that your business model can currently and realistically serve. See Segmented Addressable Market and Total Addressable Market
- **Situational Analysis:** Situational analysis often is called the foundation of a marketing plan. A situational analysis includes a thorough examination of internal and external factors affecting a business. It creates an overview of the organization that will lead to a better understanding of the factors that will influence its future. → A **SWOT Analysis** is another method under the situation analysis that examines the Strengths and Weaknesses of a company (internal environment) as well as the Opportunities and Threats within the market (external environment).
- **Stock Keeping Unit (SKU):** An identification, usually alphanumeric, of a particular product that allows it to be tracked for inventory purposes. Typically, an SKU (pronounced with the individual letters or as SKYEW) is associated with any purchasable item in a store or catalogue.
- **Small Business Administration (SBA):** Created in 1953, it is an independent agency of the U.S. federal government that aids, counsels, assists, and protects the interests of

small business.

- **Small Business Development Centers (SBDC):** SBA program using university faculty and others to provide management assistance to current and prospective small business owners.

- **Social Entrepreneur:** Someone who recognizes a social problem and uses entrepreneurial principles to organize, create, and manage a venture to make social change. Social entrepreneurs often work through non-profit organization and citizen groups, but they may also work in the private or governmental sector. Many successful entrepreneurs, such as Bill Gates of Microsoft, have become social entrepreneurs.

- **Sole Proprietorship:** A business form with one owner who is responsible for all of the firm's liabilities.

- **Stakeholder:** Any person, organization, social group, or society at large that has a stake in the business. Thus, stakeholders can be internal or external to the business. A stake is a vital interest in the business or its activities. Some examples of key stakeholders are creditors, investors, directors, employees, government (and its agencies), owners (shareholders), suppliers, unions, and the community from which the business draws its resources.

- **Startup Valuation:** Measuring the value of a startup business for investors. One of the most often asked questions to startup businessmen is, "how much is your business worth." Unfortunately, valuation is more of a science and there is little agreement about how to set a value for startup businesses. A startup company's value is largely dictated by the market forces in the industry in which it operates. Specifically, the current value is dictated by the market forces in play today and today's perception of what the future will bring.

- **Strategic Planning:** A tool used in the process of

determining how to achieved the companies long term goals.

- **Strategic Alliance:** An on-going relationship between two businesses in which they combine efforts for a specific purpose.

- **Startup:** Defined as a new business that has yet to achieve a sustainable positive cash flow or has been in operation for a limited amount of time.

- **Startup Capital:** The amount of cash needed for the new business to go from conception to production; aka seed money.

- **Start-up Financing:** Funding provided to companies for use in product development and initial marketing. It is usually funding for firms that have not yet sold their product commercially.

- **Super angel (or "super-angel") investors:** A group of serial investors in early stage ventures in Silicon Valley, California and other technology centers who are particularly sophisticated, insightful, or well-connected in the startup business community.

- **Sweat Equity:** The contribution to a project or enterprise in the form of effort and toil. Sweat equity is the ownership interest, or increase in value, that is created as a direct result of hard work by the owner(s). It is the preferred mode of building equity for cash-strapped entrepreneurs in their start-up ventures, since they may be unable to contribute much financial capital to their enterprise. In the context of real estate, sweat equity refers to value-enhancing improvements made by homeowners themselves to their properties. The term is probably derived from the fact that such equity is considered to be generated from the "sweat of one's brow."

- **SWOT Analysis:** See situational analysis

- **Systematic Risk**: Some risks facing the company are not unique to that business in that market, but are faced by all firms operating in the broader, general marketplace. These so-called "systematic" risks (such as changes in interest rate levels, the performance and direction of the U.S. economy or the availability of certain types of skilled labor) cannot be avoided.

- **Tax**: See corporate tax
- **Tax Deductions**: See deductions
- **Total Available Market (TAM)**: Or the Total Addressable Market is everyone you wish you could serve or sell your product to. Market research reveals what your total available market will be. See Segmented Addressable Market and Share of the Market.
- **Trademark**: A form of legal protection given to a business or individual for words, names, symbols, sounds, or colors that distinguish goods and services. Trademarks, unlike patents, can be renewed forever as long as they are being used in business.
- **Tribe:** A group of people connected to one another, connected to a leader, and connected to an idea.
- **Unsecured Loan:** Short-term source of borrowed capital for which the borrower does not pledge any assets as collateral.
- **Validated Learning:** A Lean Startup term meaning a process where one learns by trying out an initial idea and measuring it to validate its effect. Each test is an iteration where many more iterations follow. See Build/Measure/Learn
- **Valuation:** See startup valuation
- **Values:** See Organizational Values
- **Value Added Tax (VAT):** A tax on the amount by which the value of an article has been increased at each stage of its production or distribution. a popular way of implementing a consumption tax in Europe, Japan, and many other countries. All OECD (Organization for

Economic Co-operation and Development) countries except the United States have a value-added tax. It differs from the sales tax in that taxes are applied to the difference between the seller-purchased price and the resale price. This is accomplished by taking full tax on all sales, but refunding the tax difference to the sellers.

- **Variable Costs:** Costs that vary as the amount produced or sold varies. See also fixed costs

- **Vendor:** A person or business that supplies goods or services to a company. Another term for vendor is supplier. In many situations a company presents the vendor with a purchase order stating the goods or services needed, the price, delivery date, and other terms.

- **Venture Capital:** Capital invested in a project in which there is a substantial element of risk, typically a new or expanding business.

- **Venture Investors**: An institution specializing in the provision of large amounts of long-term capital to enterprises with a limited track record but with the expectation of substantial growth. The venture capitalist also may provide varying degrees of managerial and technical expertise.

- **Weighted Average (between debt and equity) Cost of Capital (WACC):** This is the firm's true annual cost to obtain and hold onto the combination of debt and equity that pays for the fixed asset base. Every time the owners contemplate investing in a new project, the IRR for that project must be at least equal to the WACC of the funds used to do that project, otherwise it makes no sense taking on that new project, because its return cannot even cover the cost of the capital employed to make the project happen.

- **Working Capital:** Current assets are those short-term funds represented by cash in the bank, funds parked in near-term instruments earning interest, funds tied up in inventory, and all those accounts receivable waiting to be collected. Subtracting the company's current liabilities from these current assets shows how much working capital (your firm's truest measure of liquidity) is on hand and its ability to pay for decisions in the short-term. For example, if the firm has $500,000 in current assets and $350,000 in current liabilities, then $150,000 is free and clear as working capital, available for spending on new things as needed by the company.

Appendix E

Internet Resources

Startup Power

> http://www.startuppower.co

U.S. Small Business Administration

> https://www.sba.gov/

Small Business Development Center

> http://americassbdc.org/

Service Core of Retired Executives (SCORE)

> https://www.score.org/

Entrepreneur.com

> https://www.entrepreneur.com

The Lean Startup

> http://theleanstartup.com/

The 7 Day Startup

> http://7daystartup.com/

Business News Daily

> http://www.businessnewsdaily.com/

Take Notes Here

<u>Take Notes Here</u>

Take Notes Here

Take Notes Here

Take Notes Here

Jimmy Bayes

Take Notes Here

Take Notes Here

__Take Notes Here__

Take Notes Here

Jimmy Bayes

<u>Take Notes Here</u>

Take Notes Here

Take Notes Here

Take Notes Here